Secret Chambers and Hiding Places

Also from Westphalia Press

westphaliapress.org

SECRET CHAMBERS
AND
HIDING-PLACES

*THE HISTORIC, ROMANTIC
& LEGENDARY STORIES &
TRADITIONS ABOUT HIDING-
HOLES, SECRET CHAMBERS, &c.*

By ALLAN FEA, Author of
" *The Flight of the King,*" " *King
Monmouth,*" *&c.* .   .

WITH NUMEROUS ILLUSTRATIONS
BY THE AUTHOR   .

MOSELEY HALL, STAFFORDSHIRE.

Frontispiece.]

CONTENTS

LIST OF ILLUSTRATIONS

INTRODUCTION

THE secret chamber is unrivalled even by the
haunted house for the mystery and
romance surrounding it. Volumes have been
written about the haunted house, while the secret
chamber has found but few exponents. The
ancestral ghost has had his day, and to all intents
and purposes is dead, notwithstanding the existence
of the Psychical Society and the investigations
of Mr. Stead and the late Lord Bute. "Alas!
poor ghost!" he is treated with scorn and derision
by the multitude in these advanced days of modern
enlightenment. The search-light of science has
penetrated even into his sacred haunts, until, no
longer having a leg to stand upon, he has
fallen from the exalted position he occupied for
centuries, and fallen moreover into ridicule!

In the secret chamber, however, we have something tangible to deal with—a subject not only keenly interesting from an antiquarian point of view, but one deserving the attention of the general reader ; for in exploring the gloomy hiding-holes, concealed apartments, passages, and staircases in our old halls and manor houses we probe, as it were, into the very groundwork of romance. We find actuality to support the weird and mysterious stories of fiction, which those of us who are honest enough to admit a lingering love of the marvellous must now doubly appreciate, from the fact that our school-day impressions of such things are not only revived, but are strengthened with the semblance of truth. Truly Bishop Copleston wrote : " If the things we hear told be avowedly fictitious, and yet curious or affecting or entertaining, we may indeed admire the author of the fiction, and may take pleasure in contemplating the exercise of his skill. But this is a pleasure of another kind—a pleasure wholly distinct from that which is derived from discovering what was *unknown*, or clearing up what was *doubtful*. And even when the narrative is in its own nature, such as to please us and to engage our attention, how greatly is the interest increased if we place entire confidence in its *truth*! Who has not heard from a child when listening to a tale of deep interest—who has not often heard the artless and eager question, ' Is it true?' "

From Horace Walpole, Mrs. Radcliffe, Sir Walter Scott, Dumas, Lytton, Ainsworth, Le Fanu, and Mrs. Henry Wood, down to the latest up-to-date novelists of to-day, the secret chamber (an ingenious *necessity* of the " good old times ") has afforded invaluable " property "—indeed, in many instances the whole vitality of a plot is, like its ingenious opening, hinged upon the masked wall, behind which lay concealed what hidden mysteries, what undreamed-of revelations! The thread of the story, like Fair Rosamond's silken clue, leads up to and at length reveals the buried secret, and (unlike the above comparison in this instance) all ends happily!

Bulwer Lytton honestly confesses that the spirit of romance in his novels " was greatly due to their having been written at my ancestral home, Knebworth, Herts. How could I help writing romances," he says, " after living amongst the secret panels and hiding-places of our dear old home? How often have I trembled with fear at the sound of my own footsteps when I ventured into the picture gallery! How fearfully have I glanced at the faces of my ancestors as I peered into the shadowy abysses of the ' secret chamber.' It was years before I could venture inside without my hair literally bristling with terror."

What would *Woodstock* be without the mysterious picture, *Peveril of the Peak* without the sliding panel, the Castlewood of *Esmond* without Father Holt's concealed apartments, *Twenty Years After*, *Marguerite de Valois*, *The Tower of London*, *Guy Fawkes*, and countless other novels of the same type, without the convenient contrivances of which the *dramatis personæ* make such effectual use ?

Apart, however, from the importance of the secret chamber in fiction, it is closely associated with many an important historical event. The stories of the Gunpowder Plot, Charles II.'s escape from Worcester, the Jacobite risings of 1715 and 1745, and many another stirring episode in the annals of our country, speak of the service it rendered to fugitives in the last extremity of danger. When we inspect the actual walls of these confined spaces that saved the lives of our ancestors, how vividly we can realise the hardships they must have endured ; and in wondering at the mingled ingenuity and simplicity of construction, there is also a certain amount of comfort to be derived from drawing a comparison between those troublous and our own more peaceful times.

Secret Chambers and Hiding-Places

CHAPTER I

A GREAT DEVISER OF "PRIESTS' HOLES"

DURING the deadly feuds which existed in the Middle Ages, when no man was secure from spies and traitors even within the walls of his own house, it is no matter of wonder that the castles and mansions of the powerful and wealthy were usually provided with some precaution in the event of a sudden surprise— *viz.* a secret means of concealment or escape that could be used at a moment's notice; but the majority of secret chambers and hiding-places

in our ancient buildings owe their origin to
religious persecution, particularly during the reign
of Elizabeth, when the most stringent laws
and oppressive burdens were inflicted upon all
persons who professed the tenets of the Church
of Rome.

In the first years of the virgin Queen's reign
all who clung to the older forms of the Catholic
faith were mercifully connived at, so long as they
solemnised their own religious rites within their
private dwelling-houses ; but after the Roman
Catholic rising in the north and numerous other
Popish plots, the utmost severity of the law was
enforced, particularly against seminarists, whose chief
object was, as was generally believed, to stir up
their disciples in England against the Protestant
Queen. An Act was passed prohibiting a member
of the Church of Rome from celebrating the
rites of his religion on pain of forfeiture for
the first offence, a year's imprisonment for the
second, and imprisonment for life for the

third.[1] All those who refused to take the Oath of Supremacy were called "recusants" and were guilty of high treason. A law was also enacted which provided that if any Papist should convert a Protestant to the Church of Rome, both should suffer death, as for high treason.

The sanguinary laws against seminary priests and " recusants " were enforced with the greatest severity after the discovery of the Gunpowder Plot. These were revived for a period in Charles II.'s reign, when Oates's plot worked up a fanatical hatred against all professors of the ancient faith. In the mansions of the old Roman Catholic families we often find an apartment in a secluded part of the house or garret in the roof named " the chapel," where religious rites could be performed with the utmost privacy, and close handy was usually an artfully contrived hiding-place, not only for the

---

[1] In December, 1591, a priest was hanged before the door of a house in Gray's Inn Fields for having there said Mass the month previously.

officiating priest to slip into in case of emergency, but also where the vestments, sacred vessels, and altar furniture could be put away at a moment's notice.

It appears from the writings of Father Tanner[1] that most of the hiding-places for priests, usually called "priests' holes," were invented and constructed by the Jesuit Nicholas Owen, a servant of Father Garnet, who devoted the greater part of his life to constructing these places in the principal Roman Catholic houses all over England.

"With incomparable skill," says an authority, "he knew how to conduct priests to a place of safety along subterranean passages, to hide them between walls and bury them in impenetrable recesses, and to entangle them in labyrinths and a thousand windings. But what was much more difficult of accomplishment, he so disguised the entrances to these as to make them most unlike what they really were.

[1] *Vita et Mors* (1675), p. 75.

Moreover, he kept these places so close a secret with himself that he would never disclose to another the place of concealment of any Catholic. He alone was both their architect and their builder, working at them with inexhaustible industry and labour, for generally the thickest walls had to be broken into and large stones excavated, requiring stronger arms than were attached to a body so diminutive as to give him the nickname of 'Little John,' and by this his skill many priests were preserved from the prey of persecutors. Nor is it easy to find anyone who had not often been indebted for his life to Owen's hiding-places."

I low effectually " Little John's " peculiar ingenuity baffled the exhaustive searches of the " pursuivants," or priest-hunters, has been shown by contemporary accounts of the searches that took place frequently in suspected houses. Father Gerard, in his Auto-biography, has handed down to us many curious details of the mode of procedure upon these occasions—how the search-party would bring with them skilled carpenters and masons and try every possible expedient, from systematic measurements and soundings to bodily tearing down the panelling and pulling up the floors. It was not an uncommon thing for a rigid search to last a fortnight and for the " pursuivants " to go away empty handed, while perhaps the object of the search was hidden the whole time within a wall's thickness of his pursuers, half starved, cramped and sore with prolonged confinement, and almost afraid to breathe lest the least sound should throw suspicion upon the particular spot where he lay immured.

After the discovery of the Gunpowder Plot, " Little John " and his master, Father Garnet, were arrested at Hindlip Hall, Worcestershire, from information given to the Government by Catesby's servant Bates. Cecil, who was well aware of Owen's skill in constructing hiding-places, wrote exultingly : " Great joy was caused all through the kingdom by the arrest of Owen, knowing his skill in constructing hiding-places, and the innumerable number of these dark holes which he had schemed for hiding priests throughout the kingdom." He hoped that "great booty of priests" might be taken in consequence of the secrets Owen would be made to reveal, and directed that first he should "be coaxed if he be willing to contract for his life," but that "the secret is to be wrung from him." The horrors of the rack, however, failed in its purpose. His terrible death is thus briefly recorded by the Governor of the Tower at that time : "The man is dead—he died in our hands" ; and perhaps it is as well the ghastly details did not transpire in his report.

The curious old mansion Hindlip Hall (pulled down in the early part of the last century) was erected in 1572 by John Abingdon, or Habington, whose son Thomas (the brother-in-law of Lord Monteagle) was deeply involved in the numerous plots against the reformed religion. A long

imprisonment in the Tower for his futile efforts
to set Mary Queen of Scots at liberty, far
from curing the dangerous schemes of this zealous
partisan of the luckless Stuart heroine, only kept
him out of mischief for a time. No sooner had
he obtained his freedom than he set his mind
to work to turn his house in Worcestershire into
a harbour of refuge for the followers of the older
rites. In the quaint irregularities of the masonry
free scope was given to " Little John's " ingenuity ;
indeed, there is every proof that some of his
masterpieces were constructed here. A few years
before the " Powder Plot " was discovered, it was
a hanging matter for a priest to be caught
celebrating the Mass. Yet with the facilities at
Hindlip he might do so with comfort, with every
assurance that he had the means of evading the
law. The walls of the mansion were literally
riddled with secret chambers and passages. There
was little fear of being run to earth with hidden
exits everywhere. Wainscoting, solid brickwork,

or stone hearth were equally accommodating, and would swallow up fugitives wholesale, and close over them, to " Open, Sesame ! " again only at the hider's pleasure.

CHAPTER II

HINDLIP HALL

THE capture of Father Garnet and "Little John" with two others, Hall and Chambers, at Hindlip, as detailed in a curious manuscript in the British Museum, gives us an insight into the search-proof merits of Abingdon's mansion. The document is headed : "*A true discovery of the service performed at Hindlip, the house of Mr. Thomas Abbingdon, for the apprehension of Mr. Henry Garnet, alias Wolley, provincial of the Jesuits, and other dangerous persons, there found in January last,* 1605," and runs on :—

"After the king's royal promise of bountiful reward to such as would apprehend the

HINDLIP HALL, WORCESTERSHIRE.
(*From an old Drawing.*)

traitors concerned in the Powder Conspiracy, and much expectation of subject-like duty, but no return made thereof in so important a matter, a warrant was directed to the right worthy and worshipful knight, Sir Henry Bromlie ; and the proclamation delivered therewith, describing the features and shapes of the men, for the better discovering them. He, not neglecting so a weighty a business, horsing himself with a seemly troop of his own attendants, and calling to his assistance so many as in discretion was thought meet, having likewise in his company Sir Edward Bromlie, on Monday, Jan. 20 last, by break of day, did engirt and round beat the house of Mayster Thomas Abbingdon, at Hindlip, near Worcester. Mr. Abbingdon, not being then at home, but ridden abroad about some occasions best known to himself ; the house being goodlie, and of great receipt, it required the more diligent labour and pains in the searching. It appeared there was no want ; and Mr. Abbingdon himself

coming home that night, the commission and
proclamation being shown unto him, he denied
any such men to be in his house, and voluntarily
to die at his own gate, if any such were to be
found in his house, or in that shire. But this
liberal or rather rash speech could not cause the
search so slightly to be given over ; the cause
enforced more respect than words of that or
any such like nature ; and proceeding on
according to the trust reposed in him in the
gallery over the gate there were found two
cunning and very artificial conveyances in
the main brick-wall, so ingeniously framed, and
with such art, as it cost much labour ere they
could be found. Three other secret places, contrived by no less skill and industry, were found
in and about the chimneys, in one whereof two
of the traitors were close concealed. These
chimney-conveyances being so strangely formed,
having the entrances into them so curiously
covered over with brick, mortared and made fast

to planks of wood, and coloured black, like the other parts of the chimney, that very diligent inquisition might well have passed by, without throwing the least suspicion upon such unsuspicious places. And whereas divers funnels are usually made to chimneys according as they are combined together, and serve for necessary use in several rooms, so here were some that exceeded common expectation, seeming outwardly fit for carrying forth smoke ; but being further examined and seen into, their service was to no such purpose but only to lend air and light downward into the concealments, where such as were concealed in them, at any time should be hidden. Eleven secret corners and conveyances were found in the said house, all of them having books, Massing stuff, and Popish trumpery in them, only two excepted, which appeared to have been found on former searches, and therefore had now the less credit given to them ; but Mayster Abbingdon would take no knowledge of any of these places, nor that the books, or Massing stuff, were any of his, until at length the deeds of his lands being found in one of them, whose custody doubtless he would not commit to any place of neglect, or where he should have no intelligence of them, whereto he could [not] then devise any sufficient excuse.

Three days had been wholly spent, and no man found there all this while ; but upon the fourth day, in the morning, from behind the wainscot in the galleries, came forth two men of their own voluntary accord, as being no longer able there to conceal themselves ; for they confessed that they had but one apple between them, which was all the sustenance they had received during the time they were thus hidden. One of them named Owen, who afterwards murdered himself in the Tower ; and the other Chambers ; but they would take no other knowledge of any other men's being in the house. On the eighth day the before-mentioned place in the chimney was found, according as they had all been at several times, one after another, though before set down together, for expressing the just number of them.

"Forth of this secret and most cunning conveyance came Henry Garnet, the Jesuit, sought for, and another with him, named Hall ; marmalade and other sweetmeats were found there lying by them ; but their better maintenance had been by a quill or reed, through a little hole in the chimney that backed another chimney into the gentlewoman's chamber ; and by that passage candles, broths, and warm drinks had been conveyed in unto them.

"Now in regard the place was in so close . . . and did , much annoy them that made entrance in upon them, to whom they confessed that they had not been able to hold out one whole day longer, but either they must have squeeled, or perished in the place. The whole service endured the space of eleven nights and twelve days, and no more persons being there found, in company with Mayster Abbingdon himself, Garnet, Hill [Hall], Owen, and Chambers, were brought up to London to understand further of his highness's pleasure."

That the Government had good grounds for suspecting Hindlip and its numerous hiding-places may be gathered from the official instructions the Worcestershire Justice of the Peace and his search-party had to follow. The wainscoting in the east part of the parlour and in the dining-room, being suspected of screening "a vault" or passage, was to be removed, the walls and floors were to be pierced in all directions, comparative measurements were to be taken between the upper and the lower rooms, and in particular the chimneys, and the roof had to be minutely examined and measure-ments taken, which might bring to light some unaccounted-for space that had been turned to good account by the unfortunate inventor, who was eventually starved out of one of his clever contrivances.

Only shortly before Owen had had a very narrow escape at Stoke Pogis while engaged in constructing " priests' holes " at the Manor House. The secluded position of this building adapted it for the purpose for which a Roman Catholic zealot had taken it. But this was not the only advantage. The walls were of vast thickness and offered every facility for turning them to account. While " Little John " was busily engaged burrowing into the masonry the dreaded " pursuivants " arrived ; but somehow or other he slipped between their fingers and got away under cover of the surrounding woods.

The wing of this old mansion which has survived to see the twentieth century witnessed many strange events. It has welcomed good Queen Bess, guarded the Martyr King, and refused admittance to Dutch William. A couple of centuries after it had sheltered hunted Jesuits, a

descendant of William Penn became possessed of
it, and cleared away many of the massive walls,
in some of which—who can tell ?—were locked
up secrets that the rack failed to reveal—secrets
by which Owen " *murdered himself* " ! in the
Tower !

One of the hiding-places at Hindlip, it will be
remembered, could be supplied with broth, wine,
or any liquid nourishment through a small aperture
in the wall of the adjoining room. A very good
example of such an arrangement was to be seen
until only a few years ago (when fire, alas! the
fate of so many ancestral homes, destroyed it)
at Irnham Hall, in Lincolnshire. A large
hiding-place could thus be accommodated, but
detection of the narrow iron tube by which
the imprisoned fugitive could be kept alive was
practically impossible. A solid oak beam,
forming a step between two bedrooms, concealed a panel into which the tube was cunningly
fitted, and the step was so arranged that it

could be removed and replaced with the greatest ease.[1]

The hiding-place at Irnham (which measured eight feet by five, and about five feet six inches in height) was discovered by a tell-tale chimney that was not in the least blackened by soot or smoke. This originally gave the clue to the secret, and when the shaft of the chimney was examined, it was found to lead direct to the priest's hole, to which it afforded air and light.

Had not the particular hiding-place in which Garnet and his companions sought shelter been discovered, they could well have held out the twelve days' search. As a rule, a small stock of provisions was kept in these places, as the visits of the search parties were necessarily very sudden and unexpected. The way down into these hidden quarters was from the floor above, through the

[1] Harvington Hall, mentioned hereafter, has a contrivance of this kind.

hearth of a fireplace, which could be raised and lowered like a trap-door.[1]

In a letter from Garnet to Ann Vaux, preserved in the Record Office, he thus describes his precarious situation : " After we had been in the hoale seven days and seven nights and some odd hours, every man may well think we were well wearyed, and indeed so it was, for we generally satte, save that some times we could half stretch ourselves, the place not being high eno', and we had our legges so straitened that we could not, sitting, find place for them, so that we both were in continuous paine of our legges, and both our legges, especially mine, were much swollen. We were very merry and content within, and heard the searchers every day most curious over us, which made me indeed think the place would be found. When we came forth we appeared like ghosts." [2]

There is an old timber-framed cottage near the

---

[1] See Fowlis's *Romish Treasons.*

[2] *State Papers*, Domestic (James I.).

modern mansion of Hindlip which is said to have had its share in sheltering the plotters. A room is pointed out where Digby and Catesby concealed themselves, and from one of the chimneys at some time or another a priest was captured and led to execution.

CHAPTER III

PRIEST-HUNTING AT BRADDOCKS

IN the parish of Wimbish, about six miles from Saffron Walden, stand the remains of a fine old Tudor house named Broad Oaks, or Braddocks, which in Elizabeth's reign was a noted house for priest-hunting. Wandering through its ancient rooms, the imagination readily carries us back to the drama enacted here three centuries ago with a vividness as if the events recorded had happened yesterday. "The chapel" and priests' holes may still be seen, and a fine old stone fireplace that was stripped of its overmantel, etc., of carved oak by the "pursuivants" in their vain efforts when Father Gerard was concealed in the house.

The old Essex family of Wiseman of Braddocks

BRADDOCKS, ESSEX.

FIREPLACE AT BRADDOCKS.

were staunch Romanists, and their home, being a noted resort for priests, received from time to time sudden visits. The dreaded Topcliffe had upon one occasion nearly brought the head of the family, an aged widow lady, to the horrors of the press-yard, but her punishment eventually took the form of imprisonment. Searches at Braddocks had brought forth hiding-places, priests, compromising papers, and armour and weapons. Let us see with what success the house was explored in the Easter of the year 1594.

Gerard gives his exciting experiences as follows[1] :—

" The searchers broke down the door, and forcing their way in, spread through the house with great noise and racket.

" Their first step was to lock up the mistress of the house[2] in her own room with her two

[1] See Autobiography of Father John Gerard.

[2] Jane Wiseman, wife of William Wiseman. N.B.—The late Cardinal Wiseman was descended from a junior branch of this family. See Life of Father John Gerard, by John Morris.

daughters, and the Catholic servants they kept locked up in divers places in the same part of the house.

" They then took to themselves the whole house, which was of a good size, and made a thorough search in every part, not forgetting even to look under the tiles of the roof. The darkest corners they examined with the help of candles. Finding nothing whatever they began to break down certain places that they suspected. They measured the walls with long rods, so that if they did not tally they might pierce the part not accounted for. Then they sounded the walls and all the floors to find out and break into any hollow places there might be.

" They spent two days in this work without finding anything. Thinking therefore that I had gone on Easter Sunday, the two magistrates went away on the second day, leaving the pursuivants to take the mistress of the house and all her Catholic servants of both sexes to London to be

examined and imprisoned. They meant to leave
some who were not Catholics to keep the house,
the traitor (one of the servants of the house) being
one of them.

" The good lady was pleased at this, for she
hoped that he would be the means of freeing me
and rescuing me from death ; for she knew that
I had made up my mind to suffer and die of
starvation between two walls, rather than come
forth and save my own life at the expense of
others.

" In fact, during those four days that I lay hid
I had nothing to eat but a biscuit or two and
a little quince jelly, which my hostess had at hand
and gave me as I was going in.

" She did not look for any more, as she supposed
that the search would not last beyond a day. But
now that two days were gone and she was to be
carried off on the third with all her trusty servants,
she began to be afraid of my dying of sheer hunger.
She bethought herself then of the traitor who she

heard was to be left behind. He had made a
great fuss and show of eagerness in withstanding
the searchers when they first forced their way
in. For all that she would not have let him
know of the hiding-places, had she not been in
such straits. Thinking it better, however, to rescue
me from certain death, even at some risk to herself,
she charged him, when she was taken away and
every one had gone, to go into a certain room, call
me by my wonted name, and tell me that the others
had been taken to prison, but that he was left
to deliver me. I would then answer, she said,
from behind the lath and plaster where I lay concealed. The traitor promised to obey faithfully ;
but he was faithful only to the faithless, for he
unfolded the whole matter to the ruffians who
had remained behind.

"No sooner had they heard it than they called
back the magistrates who had departed. These
returned early in the morning and renewed the
search.

"They measured and sounded everywhere much more carefully than before, especially in the chamber above mentioned, in order to find out some hollow place. But finding nothing whatever during the whole of the third day, they proposed on the morrow to strip off the wainscot of that room.

"Meanwhile, they set guards in all the rooms about to watch all night, lest I should escape. I heard from my hiding-place the password which the captain of the band gave to his soldiers, and I might have got off by using it, were it not that they would have seen me issuing from my retreat, for there were two on guard in the chapel where I got into my hiding-place, and several also in the large wainscoted room which had been pointed out to them.

"But mark the wonderful Providence of God. Here was I in my hiding-place. The way I got into it was by taking up the floor, made of wood and bricks, under the fireplace. The place was so constructed that a fire could not be lit in it without damaging the house ; though we made a point of keeping wood there, as if it were meant for a fire.

" Well, the men on the night watch lit a fire in this very grate and began chatting together close to it. Soon the bricks which had not bricks but wood underneath them got loose, and nearly fell out of their places as the wood gave way. On noticing this and probing the place with a stick, they found that the bottom was made of wood, whereupon they remarked that this was something curious. I thought that they were going there and then to break open the place and enter, but they made up their minds at last to put off further examination till next day.

" Next morning, therefore, they renewed the search most carefully, everywhere except in the top chamber which served as a chapel, and in which the two watchmen had made a fire over my head and had noticed the strange make of the grate. God had blotted out of their memory all remembrance of the thing. Nay, none of the searchers entered the place the whole day, though it was the one that was most open to suspicion, and if they had entered, they would have found me without any search ; rather, I should say, they would have seen me, for the fire had burnt a great hole in my hiding-place, and had I not got a little out of the way, the hot embers would have fallen on me.

" The searchers, forgetting or not caring about this room, busied themselves in ransacking the rooms below, in one of which I was said to be. In fact, they found the other hiding-place which I thought of going into, as I mentioned before. It was not far off, so I could hear their shouts of joy when they first found it. But after joy comes grief ; and so it was with them. The only thing that they found was a goodly store of provision laid up. Hence they may have thought that this was the place that the mistress of the house meant ; in fact, an answer might have been given from it to the call of a person in the room mentioned by her.

" They stuck to their purpose, however, of stripping off all the wainscot of the other large room. So they set a man to work near the ceiling, close to the place where I was : for the lower part of the walls was covered with tapestry, not with wainscot. So they stripped off the wainscot all round till they came again to the very place where I lay, and there they lost heart and gave up the search.

" My hiding-place was in a thick wall of the chimney behind a finely inlaid and carved mantelpiece. They could not well take the carving down without risk of breaking it. Broken, however, it would have been, and that into a thousand pieces, had they any conception that I could be concealed behind it. But knowing that there were two flues, they did not think that there could be room enough there for a man.

" Nay, before this, on the second day of the search, they had gone into the room above, and tried the fireplace through which I had got into my hole. They then got into the chimney by a ladder to sound with their hammers. One said to another in my hearing, ' Might there not be a place here for a person to get down into the wall of the chimney below by lifting up this hearth ? ' ' No,' answered one of the pursuivants, whose voice I knew, ' you could not get down that way into the chimney underneath, but there might easily be an entrance at the back of this chimney.' So saying he gave the place a knock. I was afraid that he would hear the hollow sound of the hole where I was.

" Seeing that their toil availed them nought, they thought that I had escaped somehow, and so they went away at the end of the four days, leaving the mistress and her servants free. The yet unbetrayed traitor stayed after the searchers were gone. As soon as the doors of the house were made fast, the mistress came to call me, another four days buried Lazarus, from what would have been my tomb, had the search continued a little longer. For I was all wasted and weakened as well with hunger as with want of sleep and with having to sit so long in such a narrow space. After coming out I was seen by the traitor, whose treachery was still unknown to us. He did nothing then, not even to send after the searchers, as he knew that I meant to be off before they could be recalled."

The Wisemans had another house at North End, a few miles to the south-east of Dunmow. Here were also "priests' holes," one of which (in a chimney) secreted a certain Father Brewster during a rigid search in December, 1593.[1]

Great Harrowden, near Wellingborough, the ancient seat of the Vaux family, was another notorious

[1] *State Papers*, Dom. (Eliz.), December, 1593. See also Life of Father John Gerard, p. 138.

sanctuary for persecuted recusants. Gerard spent much of his time here in apartments specially constructed for his use, and upon more than one occasion had to have recourse to the hiding-places. Some four or five years after his experiences at Braddocks he narrowly escaped his pursuers in this way ; and in 1605, when the "pursuivants" were scouring the country for him, as he was supposed to be privy to the Gunpowder Plot, he owed his life to a secret chamber at Harrowden. The search-party remained for nine days. Night and day men were posted round the house, and every approach was guarded within a radius of three miles. With the hope of getting rid of her unwelcome guests, Lady Vaux revealed one of the "priests' holes" to prove there was nothing in her house beyond a few prohibited books ; but this did not have the desired effect, so the unfortunate inmate of the hiding-place had to continue in a cramped position, there being no room to stand up, for four or five days more. His hostess, however, managed to bring him food,

and moments were seized during the latter days
of the search to get him out that he might warm
his benumbed limbs by a fire. While these
things were going on at Harrowden, another priest,
little thinking into whose hands the well-known
sanctuary had fallen, came thither to seek shelter ;
but was seized and carried to an inn, whence
it was intended he should be removed to London
on the following day. But he managed to outwit
his captors. To evade suspicion he threw off his
cloak and sword, and under a pretext of giving
his horse drink at a stream close by the stable,
seized a lucky moment, mounted, and dashed into
the water, swam across, and galloped off to the
nearest house that could offer the convenience of a
hiding-place.[1]

At Hackney the Vaux family had another
residence with its chapel and "priest's hole," the
latter having a masked entrance high up in the
wall, which led to a space under a gable projection

[1] See Life of John Gerard, p. 386.

of the roof. For double security this contained yet an inner hiding-place. In the existing Brooke House are incorporated the modernised remains of this mansion.

CHAPTER IV

THE GUNPOWDER PLOT CONSPIRATORS

LORD VAUX of Harrowden, Sir William Catesby of Ashby St. Ledgers, and Sir Thomas Tresham of Rushton Hall (all in Northamptonshire) were upon more than one occasion arraigned before the Court of the Star Chamber for harbouring Jesuits. The old mansions Ashby St. Ledgers and Rushton fortunately still remain intact and preserve many traditions of Romanist plots. Sir William Catesby's son Robert, the chief conspirator, is said to have held secret meetings in the curious oak-panelled room over the gate-house of the former, which goes by the name of " the Plot Room." Once upon a time it was provided with a secret means of escape. At Rushton Hall a hiding-place was discovered in 1832 behind a lintel over a

ASHBY ST. LEDGERS, NORTHAMPTONSHIRE.

THE PLOT ROOM, ASHBY ST. LEDGERS.

doorway; it was full of bundles of manuscripts, prohibited books, and incriminating correspondence of the conspirator Tresham. Another place of concealment was situated in the chimney of the great hall, and in this Father Oldcorn was hidden for a time. Gayhurst, or Gothurst, in Buckinghamshire, the seat of Sir Everard Digby, also remains intact, one of the finest late Tudor buildings in the country; unfortunately, however, only recently a remarkable "priest's hole" that was here has been destroyed in consequence of modern improvements. It was a double hiding-place, one situated beneath the other; the lower one being so arranged as to receive light and air from the bottom portion of a large mullioned window—a most ingenious device. A secret passage in the hall had communication with it, and entrance was obtained through part of the flooring of an apartment, the movable part of the boards revolving upon pivots and sufficiently solid to vanquish any suspicion as to a hollow space beneath.

As may be supposed, tradition says that at the
time of Digby's arrest he was dragged forth from
this hole, but history shows that he was taken
prisoner at Holbeach House (where, it will be
remembered, the conspirators Catesby and Percy
were shot), and led to execution.   For a time
Digby sought security at Coughton Court, the
seat of the Throckmortons, in Warwickshire.
The house of this old Roman Catholic family, of
course, had its hiding-holes, one of which remains to
this day.   Holbeach as well as Hagley Hall, the
homes of the Littletons, have been rebuilt.   The
latter was pulled down in the middle of the eighteenth
century.   Here it was that Stephen Littleton and
Robert Winter were captured through the treachery
of the cook.   Grant's house, Norbrook, in Warwickshire, has also given way to a modern one.

Ambrose Rookwood's seat, Coldham Hall, near
Bury St. Edmunds, exists and retains its secret
chapel and hiding-places.   There are three of the
latter ; one of them, now a small withdrawing-

room, is entered from the oak wainscoted hall. When the house was in the market a few years ago, the "priests' holes" duly figured in the advertisements with the rest of the apartments and offices. It read a little odd, this juxtaposition of modern conveniences with what is essentially romantic, and we simply mention the fact to show that the auctioneer is well aware of the monetary value of such things.

At the time of the Gunpowder Conspiracy Rookwood rented Clopton Hall, near Stratford-on-Avon. This house also has its little chapel in the roof with adjacent "priests' holes," but many alterations have taken place from time to time. Who does not remember William Howitt's delightful description—or, to be correct, the description of a lady correspondent—of the old mansion before these restorations. "There was the old Catholic chapel," she wrote, "with a chaplain's room which had been walled up and forgotten till within the last few years. I went in on my hands and knees, for the entrance was very low. I recollect little in the chapel; but in the chaplain's room were old and I should think rare editions of many books, mostly folios. A large yellow paper copy of Dryden's *All for Love, or the World Well Lost*, date 1686, caught my eye, and is the only one I particularly remember."[1]

Huddington Court, the picturesque old home of the Winters (of whom Robert and Thomas lost their lives for their share in the Plot), stands a few miles from Droitwich. A considerable quantity of arms and ammunition were stored in the hiding-places here in 1605 in readiness for a general rising.

Two other houses may be mentioned in connection with the memorable Plot—houses that were rented by the conspirators as convenient places of rendezvous an account of their hiding-places and masked exits for escape. One of them stood in the vicinity of the Strand, in the fields behind

[1] Howitt's *Visits to Remarkable Places*.

HUDDINGTON COURT, WORCESTERSHIRE.

St. Clement's Inn. Father Gerard had taken it
some time previous to the discovery of the Plot,
and with Owen's aid some very secure hiding-places
were arranged. This he had done with two or
three other London residences, so that he and his
brother priests might use them upon hazardous
occasions ; and to one of these he owed his life
when the hue and cry after him was at its highest
pitch. By removing from one to the other they
avoided detection, though they had many narrow
escapes. One priest was celebrating Mass when
the Lord Mayor and constables suddenly burst
in. But the surprise party was disappointed :
nothing could be detected beyond the smoke of
the extinguished candles ; and in addition to the
hole where the fugitive crouched there were two
other secret chambers, neither of which was discovered. On another occasion a priest was left
shut up in a wall ; his friends were taken prisoners,
and he was in danger of starvation, until at length
he was rescued from his perilous position, carried

to one of the other houses, and again immured in the vault or chimney.

The other house was " White Webb's," on the confines of Enfield Chase. In the Record Office there is a document describing how, many Popish books and relics were discovered when the latter was searched. The building was full of trap-doors and secret passages. Some vestiges of the out-buildings of " White Webb's " may still be seen in a quaint little inn called " The King and Tinker."

But of all the narrow escapes perhaps Father Blount's experiences at Scotney Castle were the most thrilling. This old house of the Darrells, situated on the border of Kent and Sussex, like Hindlip and Braddocks and most of the residences of the Roman Catholic gentry, contained the usual lurking-places for priests. The structure as it now stands is in the main modern, having undergone from time to time considerable alterations. A vivid account of Blount's hazardous escape here

is preserved among the muniments at Stonyhurst
—a transcript of the original formerly at St. Omers.

One Christmas night towards the close of
Elizabeth's reign the castle was seized by a party
of priest-hunters, who, with their usual mode of
procedure, locked up the members of the family
securely before starting on their operations. In
the inner quadrangle of the mansion was a very
remarkable and ingenious device. A large stone
of the solid wall could be pushed aside. Though
of immense weight, it was so nicely balanced
and adjusted that it required only a slight pressure
upon one side to effect an entrance to the hiding-
place within. Those who have visited the grounds
at Chatsworth may remember a huge piece of
solid rock which can be swung round in the same
easy manner. Upon the approach of the enemy,
Father Blount and his servant hastened to the
courtyard and entered the vault; but in their
hurry to close the weighty door a small portion
of one of their girdles got jammed in, so that a

part was visible from the outside. Fortunately for the fugitives, someone in the secret, in passing the spot, happened to catch sight of this tell-tale fragment and immediately cut it off; but as a particle still showed, they called gently to those within to endeavour to pull it in, which they eventually succeeded in doing.

At this moment the pursuivants were at work in another part of the castle, but hearing the voice in the courtyard, rushed into it and commenced battering the walls, and at times upon the very door of the hiding-place, which would have given way had not those within put their combined weight against it to keep it from yielding. It was a pitchy dark night, and it was pelting with rain, so after a time, discouraged at finding nothing and wet to the skin, the soldiers put off further search until the following morning, and proceeded to dry and refresh themselves by the fire in the great hall.

When all was at rest, Father Blount and his

man, not caring to risk another day's hunting, cautiously crept forth bare-footed, and after managing to scale some high walls, dropt into the moat and swam across. And it was as well for them that they decided to quit their hiding-hole, for next morning it was discovered.

The fugitives found temporary security at another recusant house a few miles from Scotney, possibly the old half-timber house of Twissenden, where a secret chapel and adjacent "priests' holes" are still pointed out.

The original manuscript account of the search at Scotney was written by one of the Darrell family, who was in the castle at the time of the events recorded.[1]

[1] See Morris's *Troubles of our Catholic Forefathers.*

CHAPTER V

HARVINGTON, UFTON, AND INGATESTONE

WE will now go in search of some of the
most curious hiding-places in existence.
There are numerous known examples all over
the country, and perhaps as many again exist,
which will preserve their secret for ever. For
more than three hundred years they have remained
buried, and unless some accident reveals their
locked-up mysteries, they will crumble away with
the walls which contain them ; unless, indeed, fire,
the doom of so many of our ancestral halls,
reduces them to ashes and swallows up the weird
stories they might have told. In many cases not
until an ancient building is pulled down are such
strange discoveries made ; but, alas ! there are as

ENTRANCE TO "PRIEST'S HOLE," HARVINGTON HALL.

HARVINGTON HALL, WORCESTERSHIRE.

many instances where structural alterations have wantonly destroyed these interesting historical landmarks.

Unaccounted-for spaces, when detected, are readily utilised. Passages are bodily run through the heart of many a secret device, with little veneration for the mechanical ingenuity that has been displayed in their construction. The builder of to-day, as a rule, knows nothing of and cares less for such things, and so they are swept away without a thought. To such vandals we can only emphasise the remarks we have already made about the market value of a "priest-hole" nowadays.

A little to the right of the Kidderminster road, and about two miles from the pretty village of Chaddesley Corbet, with its old timber houses and inn, stands the ghostly old hall of Harvington. The ancient red-brick pile rises out of its reed-grown moat with that air of mystery which age and seeming neglect only can impart. Coming upon it unexpectedly, especially towards dusk, one is struck with the strange, dignified melancholy pervading it. Surely Hood's *Haunted House* or Poe's *House of Usher* stands before us, and we cannot get away from the impression that a mystery is wrapped within its walls. Harvington Hall dates from the reign of Henry VIII., but it has undergone various changes, so it is difficult to affix any particular period or style to its architecture ; indeed, it is this medley of different styles which forms such a poetically picturesque outline. In its day Harvington could doubtless hold its own with the finest mansions in the country, but now it is forgotten, deserted, and crumbling to pieces. Its very history appears to be lost to the world, as those who go to the county histories and general topographical works for information will find.

Inside the mansion, like the exterior, the hand of decay is perceptible on every side ; the rooms are ruined, the windows broken, the floors unsafe (excepting, by the way, a small portion of the building which is habitable). A ponderous broad oak staircase leads to a dismantled state-room, shorn of the principal part of its panelling, carving, and chimney-pieces.[1] Other desolate apartments retain their names as if in mockery ; "the drawing-room," "the chapel," "Lady Yates's nursery," and so forth. At the top of the staircase, however, we must look around carefully, for beneath the stairs is a remarkable hiding-place.

With a slight stretch of the imagination we can see an indistinct form stealthily remove the floor-board of one of the stairs and creep beneath it. This particular step of a short flight running from the landing into a garret is, upon closer inspection, indeed movable, and beneath gapes a dark cavity about five feet square, on the floor of which still remains the piece of sedge matting whereon a certain Father Wall rested his aching

[1] Most of the interior fittings were removed to Coughton Court, Warwickshire.

limbs a few days prior to his capture and
execution in August, 1679. The unfortunate man
was taken at Rushock Court, a few miles away
where he was traced after leaving Harvington.
There is a communication between the hiding-place
and " the banqueting-room " through a small concealed aperture in the wainscoting large enough to
admit of a tube, through which a straw could be
thrust for the unhappy occupant to suck up any
liquid his friends might be able to supply.

In a gloomy corridor leading from the tower
to " the reception-room " is another " priest's
hole " beneath the floor, and entered by a trap-
door artfully hidden in the boards ; this black
recess is some seven feet in depth, and can be made
secure from within. Supposing the searchers had
tracked a fugitive priest as far as this corridor,
the odds are in favour that they would have passed
over his head in their haste to reach the tower,
where they would make sure, in their own minds
at least, of discovering him. Again, here there is

UFTON COURT, BERKSHIRE.

a communication with the outside world. An oblong aperture in the top oak beam of the entrance gateway to the house, measuring about four inches across, is the secret opening—small enough to escape the most inquisitive eye, yet large enough to allow of a written note to pass between the captive and those upon the alert watching his interests.[1]

A subterranean passage is said to run under the moat from a former hiding-place, but this is doubtful ; at any rate, there are no evidences of it nowadays.

Altogether, Harvington is far from cheerful, even to a pond hard by called "Gallows Pool" ! The tragic legend associated with this is beyond the province of the present work, so we will bid adieu to this weird old hall, and turn our attention to another obscure house situated in the south-east corner of Berkshire.

[1] N.B.—In addition to the above hiding-places at Harvington, one was discovered so recently as 1894 ; at least, so we have been informed. This was some years after our visit to the old Hall.

The curious, many-gabled mansion Ufton Court,
both from its secluded situation and quaint internal
construction, appears to have been peculiarly suitable
for the secretion of persecuted priests. Here are
ample means for concealment and escape into the
surrounding woods; and so carefully have the
ingenious bolts and locks of the various hiding-
places been preserved, that one would almost
imagine that there was still actual necessity for
their use in these matter-of-fact days!

A remarkable place for concealment exists in one
of the gables close to the ceiling. It is triangular
in shape, and is opened by a spring-bolt that can
be unlatched by pulling a string which runs through
a tiny hole pierced in the framework of the door
of the adjoining room. The door of the hiding-
place swings upon a pivot, and externally is thickly
covered with plaster, so as to resemble the rest of
the wall, and is so solid that when sounded there
is no hollow sound from the cavity behind, where, no
doubt, the crucifix and sacred vessels were secreted.

HIDING-PLACE, UFTON COURT.

HIDING-PLACE, UFTON COURT.

Not far off, in an upper garret, is a hiding-place
in the thickness of the wall, large enough to
contain a man standing upright. Like the other,
the door, or entrance, forms part of the plaster
wall, intersected by thick oak beams, into which
it exactly fits, disguising any appearance of an
opening. Again, in one of the passages of this
curious old mansion are further evidences of the
hardships to which Romish priests were subjected—
a trap in the floor, which can only be opened by
pulling up what exteriorly appears to be the head
of one of the nails of the flooring ; by raising this
a spring is released and a trap-door opened, revealing a large hole with a narrow ladder leading
down into it. When this hiding-place was
discovered in 1830, its contents were significant—
viz. a crucifix and two ancient petronels.
Apartments known as " the chapel " and " the
priest's vestry " are still pointed out. The walls
throughout the house appear to be intersected with
passages and masked spaces, and old residents

claim to have worked their way by these means right through from the garrets to the basement, though now the several hiding-places do not communicate one with another. There are said to be no less than twelve places of concealment in various parts of the building. A shaft in the cellar is supposed to be one of the means of exit from " the dining-room," and at the back of the house a subterranean passage may still be traced a considerable distance under the terrace.

An interesting discovery was made some years ago at Ingatestone Hall, Essex, the ancient seat of the Petres. The late Rev. Canon Last, who had resided there as private chaplain for over sixty years, described to us the incidents of this curious " find," to which he was an eye-witness. Some of the floor-boards in the south-east corner of a small ante-room adjoining what was once " the host's bedroom," facing the south front, broke away, rotten with age, while some children were playing there. These being removed, a second layer of

INGATESTONE HALL, ESSEX.

INGATESTONE HALL.

boards was brought to light within a foot of the
old flooring, and in this a trap-door was found
which, when opened, discovered a large "priest's
hole," measuring fourteen feet long, ten feet high,
and two feet wide. A twelve-step ladder led down
into it, and the floor being on a level with the
basement of the house was covered with a layer
of dry sand to the depth of nearly a foot, so as
to absorb any moisture from the ground.[1]   In
the sand a few bones of a bird were found,
possibly the remains of food supplied to some
unfortunate priest. Those who climb down into
this hole will find much that is interesting to
repay them their trouble. From the wall projects
a candle-holder, rudely modelled out of clay. An
examination of the brick-work in the interior of
the "priest's hole" proves it to be of later con-

[1] At Moorcroft House, near Hillingdon, Middlesex, now
modernised and occupied as a private lunatic asylum, ten priests
were once concealed for four days in a hiding-place, the floor of
which was covered some inches in water. This was one of the
many comforts of a "priest's hole"!

struction than the rest of the house (which dates from the early part of the sixteenth century), so in all likelihood " Little John " was the manufacturer.

Standing in the same position as when first opened, and supported by two blocks of oak, is an old chest or packing-case made of yew, covered with leather, and bound with bands of iron, wherein formerly the vestments, utensils, etc., for the Mass were kept. Upon it, in faded and antiquated writing, was the following direction : " For the Right Hon. the Lady Petre at Ingatestone Hall, in Essex." The Petres had quitted the old mansion as a residence for considerably over a century when the discovery was made.

COMPTON WINYATES WARWICKSHIRE.

CHAPTER VI

COMPTON WINYATES, SALFORD PRIOR,
SAWSTON, OXBURGH, PARHAM, PAXHILL, ETC.

OF all the ancient mansions in the United
Kingdom, and there is still, happily, a large
selection, none perhaps is so picturesque and quaintly
original in its architecture as the secluded Warwickshire house Compton Winyates. The general impression of its vast complication of gable ends
and twisted chimneys is that some enchanted palace
has found its way out of one of the fairy-tale books
of our early youth and concealed itself deep down
in a sequestered hollow among the woods and hills.
We say concealed itself, for indeed it is no easy
matter to find it, for anything in the shape of a
road seems rather to lead *away from*, than *to* it ;

indeed, there is no direct road from anywhere, and if we are fortunate enough to alight upon a footpath, that also in a very short time fades away into oblivion! So solitary also is the valley in which the mansion lies and so shut in with thick, clustering trees, that one unacquainted with the locality might pass within fifty yards of it over and over again without observing a trace of it. When, however, we do discover the beautiful old structure, we are well repaid for what trouble we may have encountered. To locate the spot within a couple of miles, we may state that Brailes is its nearest village ; the nearest town is Banbury, some nine miles away to the east.

Perhaps if we were to analyse the peculiar charm this venerable pile conveys, we should find that it is the wonderful *colour*, the harmonies of greys and greens and reds which pervade its countless chimney clusters and curious step-gables. We will be content, however, with the fascinating results, no matter how accomplished, without inquiring into the

SCOTNEY CASTLE, SUSSEX.
(*From an old Drawing.*)

COMPTON WINYATES, WARWICKSHIRE.

why and wherefore ; and pondering over the possi-
bilities of the marvellous in such a building see if
the interior can carry out such a supposition.

Wending our way to the top of the house, past
countless old-world rooms and corridors, we soon
discover evidences of the days of priest-hunting.
A " Protestant" chapel is on the ground floor (with a
grotesquely carved screen of great beauty), but up
in the roof we discover another—a " Popish " chapel.
From this there are numerous ways of escape, by
staircases and passages leading in all directions,
for even in the almost impenetrable seclusion
of this house the profoundest secrecy was necessary
for those who wished to celebrate the rites of
the forbidden religion. Should the priest be
surprised and not have time to descend one of the
many staircases and effect his escape by the ready
means in the lower part of the house, there are
secret closets between the timber beams of the roof
and the wainscot into which he could creep.

Curious rooms run along each side in the roof

round the quadrangle, called "the barracks," into which it would be possible to pack away a whole regiment of soldiers. Not far away are "the false floors," a typical Amy Robsart death-trap!

A place of security here, once upon a time, could only be reached by a ladder; later, however, it was made easier of access by a dark passage, but it was as secure as ever from intrusion. The fugitive had the ready means of isolating himself by removing a large portion of the floor-boards; supposing, therefore, his lurking-place had been traced, he had only to arrange this deadly gap, and his pursuers would run headlong to their fate.

Many other strange rooms there are, not the least interesting of which is a tiny apartment away from everywhere called "the Devil's chamber," and another little chamber whose window is *invariably found open in the morning, though securely fastened on the previous night!*

Various finds have been made from time to time at Compton Winyates. Not many years ago a

THE MINSTRELS' GALLERY, COMPTON WINYATES

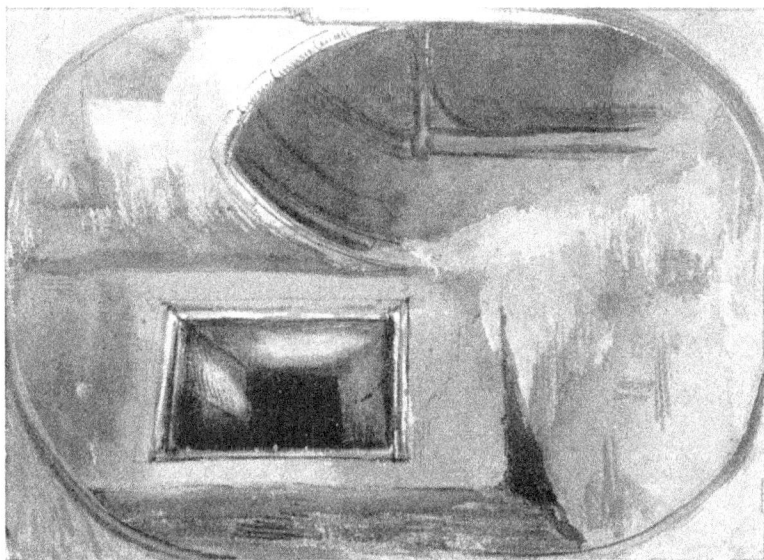

HIDING-PLACE, COMPTON WINYATES.

bricked-up space was found in a wall containing a perfect skeleton !—at another an antique box full of papers belonging to the past history of the family (the Comptons) was discovered in a secret cavity beneath one of the windows.

The " false floors " to which we have alluded suggests a hiding-place that was put to very practical use by two old maiden ladies some years ago at an ancient building near Malvern, Pickersleigh Court. Each night before retiring to rest some floor-boards of a passage, originally the entrance to a " priest's hole," were removed. This passage led to their bedroom, so that they were protected much in the same way as the fugitive at Compton Winyates, by a yawning gap. Local tradition does not record how many would-be burglars were trapped in this way, but it is certain that should anyone ever have ventured along that passage, they would have been precipitated with more speed than ceremony into a cellar below. Pickersleigh, it may be pointed out, is

erroneously shown in connection with the wanderings of Charles II. after the battle of
Worcester.[1]

Salford Prior Hall (otherwise known as "the
Nunnery," or Abbots Salford), not far from
Evesham, is another mansion remarkable for its
picturesqueness as well as for its capacity for hiding.
It not only has its Roman Catholic chapel, but a
resident priest holds services there to this day.
Up in the garret is the "priest's hole," ready, it
would seem, for some present emergency, so well
is it concealed and in such perfect working order ;
and even when its position is pointed out, nothing
is to be seen but the most innocent-looking of
cupboards. By removing a hidden peg, however,
the whole back of it, shelves and all, swings
backwards into a dismal recess some four feet in
depth. This deceitful swing door may be secured
on the inside by a stout wooden bolt provided
for that purpose.

[1] See *The Flight of the King.*

PICKERSLEIGH COURT, WORCESTERSHIRE.

SAWSTON HALL, CAMBRIDGESHIRE.

"PRIEST'S HOLE," SAWSTON HALL.

SAWSTON HALL.

SALFORD PRIOR HALL, WARWICKSHIRE.

HIDING-PLACE, SALFORD PRIOR.

SHOWING ENTRANCE TO HIDING-PLACE, SALFORD PRIOR

Another hiding place as artfully contrived and as little changed since the day it was manufactured is one at Sawston, the ancestral seat of the old family of Huddleston. Sawston Hall is a typical Elizabethan building. The one which preceded it was burnt to the ground by the adherents of Lady Jane Grey, as the Huddleston of that day, upon the death of King Edward VI., received his sister Mary under his protection, and contrived her escape to Framlingham Castle, where she was carried in disguise, riding pillion behind a servant.

The secret chamber, as at Harvington, is on the top landing of the staircase, and the entrance is so cleverly arranged that it slants into the masonry of a circular tower without showing the least perceptible sign from the exterior of a space capable of holding a baby, far less a man. A particular board in the landing is raised, and beneath it, in a corner of the cavity, is found a stone slab containing a circular aperture, something after

the manner of our modern urban receptacles for
coal. From this hole a tunnel slants downwards
at an angle into the adjacent wall, where there
is an apartment some twelve feet in depth, and
wide enough to contain half a dozen people—
that is to say, not bulky ones, for the circular
entrance is far from large. Blocks of oak fixed
upon the inside of the movable floor-board fit
with great nicety into their firm oak sockets in
the beams, which run at right angles and support
the landing, so that the opening is so massive
and firm that, unless pointed out, the particular
floor-board could never be detected, and when
secured from the inside would defy a battering-
ram.

The Huddlestons, or rather their connections
the Thornboroughs, have an old house at Leyburn,
in Yorkshire, named "The Grove," which also
contained its hiding-place, but unfortunately this
is one of those instances where alterations and
modern conveniences have destroyed what can

THE KINGS' CHAMBER, OXBURGH HALL.

never be replaced. The priest, Father John Huddleston (who aided King Charles II. to escape, and who, it will be remembered, was introduced to that monarch's death-bed by way of a *secret staircase* in the palace of Whitehall), lived in this house some time during the seventeenth century.

One of the most ingenious hiding-places extant is to be seen at Oxburgh Hall, near Stoke Ferry, the grand old moated mansion of the ancient Bedingfield family. In solidity and compactness it is unique. Up in one of the turrets of the entrance gateway is a tiny closet, the floor of which is composed of brickwork fixed into a wooden frame. Upon pressure being applied to one side of this floor, the opposite side heaves up with a groan at its own weight. Beneath lies a hollow, seven feet square, where a priest might lie concealed with the gratifying knowledge that, however the ponderous trap-door be hammered from above, there would be no tell-tale hollowness

as a response. Having bolted himself in, he
might to all intents and purposes be imbedded
in a rock (though truly a toad so situated is not
always safe from intrusion). Three centuries have
rolled away and thirteen sovereigns have reigned
since the construction of this hiding-place, but
the mechanism of this masterpiece of ingenuity
remains as perfect as if it had been made yesterday!
Those who may be privileged with permission to
inspect the interesting hall will find other surprises
where least expected. An oak-panelled passage
upon the basement of the aforesaid entrance
gateway contains a secret door that gives admittance into the living-rooms in the most eccentric
manner.

A priest's hole beneath the floor of a small
oratory adjoining " the chapel " (now a bedroom)
at Borwick Hall, Lancashire, has an opening devised
much in the same fashion as that at Oxburgh.
By leaning his weight upon a certain portion of
the boards, a fugitive could slide into a convenient

ENTRANCE TO HIDING-PLACE, PARHAM HALL.

gap, while the floor would adjust itself above his head and leave no trace of his whereabouts.

Window-seats not uncommonly formed the entrance to holes beneath the level of the floor. In the long gallery of Parham Hall, Sussex, an example of this may be seen. It is not far from " the chapel," and the officiating priest in this instance would withdraw a panel whose position is now occupied by a door ; but the entrance to the hiding-place within the projecting bay of the window is much the same as it ever was. After the failure of the Babington conspiracy one Charles Paget was concealed here for some days.

The Tudor house of Tusmore, in Oxfordshire, also had a secret chamber, approached through a fixed settle in " the parlour " window. A tradition in the neighbourhood says that the great fish-pond near the site of the old house was dug by a priest and his servant in the days of religious

6

persecution, constituting their daily occupation for twelve years!

Paxhill, in Sussex, the ancient seat of the Bordes, has a priest's hole behind a window-shutter, and it is large enough to hold several persons; there is another large hiding-hole in the ceiling of a room on the ground floor, which is reached through a trap-door in the floor above. It is provided with a stone bench.

In castles and even ecclesiastical buildings sections of massive stone columns have been found to rotate and reveal a hole in an adjacent wall— even an altar has occasionally been put to use for concealing purposes. At Naworth Castle, for instance, in "Lord William's Tower," there is an oratory behind the altar, in which fugitives not only could be hidden but could see anything that transpired in its vicinity. In Chichester Cathedral there is a room called Lollards' Prison, which is approached by a sliding panel in the old consistory-room situated over the south porch. The manor

PAXHILL, SUSSEX.

CLEEVE PRIOR MANOR HOUSE, WORCESTERSHIRE.

house of Great Chalfield, in Wiltshire, has a unique device by which any suspected person could be watched. The eye of a stone mask in the masonry is hollowed out and through this a suspicious lord of the manor could, unseen, be a witness to any treachery on the part of his retainers or guests.

The old moated hall Baddesley Clinton, in Warwickshire, the ancient seat of the Ferrers, has a stone well or shaft near " the chapel." There were formerly projections or steps by which a fugitive could reach a secret passage extending round nearly two sides of the house to a small water-gate by the moat, where a boat was kept in readiness. Adjoining the " banqueting-room " on the east side of the building is a secret chamber six feet square with a bench all round it. It is now walled up, but the narrow staircase, behind the wainscoting, leading up to it is unaltered.

Cleeve Prior Manor House, in Worcestershire

(though close upon the border of Warwickshire), famous for its unique yew avenue, has a priest's hole, a cramped space five feet by two, in which it is necessary to lie down. As at Ingatestone, it is below the floor of a small chamber adjoining the principal bedroom, and is entered by removing one of the floor-boards.

Wollas Hall, an Elizabethan mansion on Bredon Hill, near Pershore (held uninterruptedly by the Hanford family since the sixteenth century), has a chapel in the upper part of the house, and a secret chamber, or priest's hole, provided with a diminutive fire-place. When the officiating priest was about to celebrate Mass, it was the custom here to spread linen upon the hedges as a sign to those in the adjacent villages who wished to attend.

A hiding-place at Treago, Herefordshire (an unique specimen of a thirteenth-century fortified mansion, inhabited by the Mynor family for more than four hundred years), has quite luxurious

BADDESLEY CLINTON HALL, WARWICKSHIRE.

accommodation—a sleeping-place and a reading-desk. It is called "Pope's Hole." The walls on the south-east side of the house are of immense thickness, and there are many indications of secret passages within them.

Some fifty years ago a hiding-hole was opened in a chimney adjoining "the chapel" of Lydiate Hall, Lancashire; and since then one was discovered behind the rafters of the roof. Another ancient house close by contained a priest's hole where were found some religious books and an old carved oak chair.

Myddleton Lodge, near Ilkley, had a secret chapel in the roof, which is now divided up into several apartments. In the grounds is to be seen a curious maze of thickly planted evergreens in the shape of a cross. From the fact that at one end remain three wooden crosses, there is but little doubt that at the time of religious persecution the privacy of the maze was used for secret worship.

When Slindon House, Sussex, was undergoing some restorations, a "priest's hole" communicating with the roof was discovered. It contained some ancient devotional books, and against the walls were hung stout leathern straps, by which a person could let himself down.

The internal arrangements at Plowden Hall, Shropshire, give one a good idea of the feeling of insecurity that must have been so prevalent in those "good old days." Running from the top of the house there is in the thickness of the wall, a concealed circular shoot about a couple of feet in diameter, through which a person could lower himself, if necessary, to the ground floor by the aid of a rope. Here also, beneath the floorboards of a cupboard in one of the bedrooms, is a concealed chamber with a fixed shelf, presumably provided to act as a sort of table for the unfortunate individual who was forced to occupy the narrow limits of the room. Years before this hiding-place was opened to the light of day (in the course of some alterations to the house), its existence and actual position was well known ; still, strange to say, the way into it had never been discovered.

CHAPTER VII

KING-HUNTING: BOSCOBEL, MOSELEY, TRENT, AND HEALE

WHEN the Civil War was raging, many a defeated cavalier owed his preservation to the "priests' holes" and secret chambers of the old Roman Catholic houses all over the country. Did not Charles II. himself owe his life to the conveniences offered at Boscobel, Moseley, Trent, and Heale? We have elsewhere [1] gone minutely into the young king's hair-breadth adventures ; but the story is so closely connected with the present subject that we must record something of his sojourn at these four old houses, as from an historical point of view they are of exceptional interest, if one but con-

[1] See *The Flight of the King*.

INTERIOR OF HIDING-PLACE, BOSCOBEL, SALOP.

.

HIDING-PLACE, BOSCOBEL, SALOP.

"PRIEST'S HOLE," BOSCOBEL, SALOP.

BOSCOBEL, SALOP.

HIDING-PLACE, TRENT HOUSE.

ENTRANCE TO HIDING-PLACE, TRENT HOUSE.

TRENT HOUSE IN 1864.

HEALE HOUSE, WILTSHIRE.

siders how the order of things would have been changed had either of these hiding-places been discovered at the time " his Sacred Majesty " occupied them. It is vain to speculate upon the probabilities; still, there is no ignoring the fact that had Charles been captured he would have shared the fate of his father.

After the defeat of Wigan, the gallant Earl of Derby sought refuge at the isolated, wood-surrounded hunting-lodge of Boscobel, and after remaining there concealed for two days, proceeded to Gatacre Park, now rebuilt, but then and for long after famous for its secret chambers. Here he remained hidden prior to the disastrous battle of Worcester.

Upon the close of that eventful third of September, 1651, the Earl, at the time that the King and his advisers knew not which way to turn for safety, recounted his recent experiences, and called attention to the loyalty of the brothers Penderel. It was speedily resolved, therefore, to

hasten northwards towards Brewood Forest, upon
the borders of Staffordshire and Salop. "As soon
as I was disguised," says Charles, "I took with me
a country fellow whose name was Richard Penderell.
. . . He was a Roman Catholic, and I chose to trust
them [the Penderells] because I knew they had hiding-
holes for priests that I thought I might make use
of in case of need." Before taking up his quarters
in the house, however, the idea of escaping into
Wales occured to Charles, so, when night set in, he
quitted Boscobel Wood, where he had been hidden
all the day, and started on foot with his rustic
guide in a westerly direction with the object of
getting over the river Severn, but various hardships and obstacles induced Penderel to suggest
a halt at a house at Madeley, near the river,
where they might rest during the day and continue
the journey under cover of darkness on the
following night ; the house further had the attrac-
tion of "priests' holes." "We continued our way
on to the village upon the Severn," resumes the

MADELEY COURT, SHROPSHIRE.

MADELEY COURT.

MADELEY COURT.

King, " where the fellow told me there was an honest gentleman, one Mr. Woolfe, that lived in that town, where I might be with great safety, for he had hiding-holes for priests. . . . So I came into the house a back way, where I found Mr. Woolfe, an old gentleman, who told me he was very sorry to see me there, because there was two companies of the militia foot at that time in arms in the town, and kept a guard at the ferry, to examine everybody that came that way in expectation of catching some that might be making their escape that way ; and that he durst not put me into any of the hiding-holes of his house, because they had been discovered, and consequently, if any search should be made, they would certainly repair to these holes, and that therefore I had no other way of security but to go into his barn and there lie behind his corn and hay."

The Madeley " priest's hole " which was considered unsafe is still extant. It is in one of the

attics of "the Upper House," but the entrance
is now very palpable.   Those who are curious
enough to climb up into this black hole will
discover a rude wooden bench within it—a
luxury compared with some hiding-places !

The river Severn being strictly guarded everywhere, Charles and his companions retraced their
steps the next night towards Boscobel.

After a day spent up in the branches of the famous
Royal Oak, the fugitive monarch made his resting-
place the secret chamber behind the wainscoting of
what is called "the Squire's Bedroom."   There is
another hiding-place, however, hard by in a garret
which may have been the one selected.   The latter
lies beneath the floor of this garret, or "Popish
chapel," as it was once termed.   At the top
of a flight of steps leading to it is a small trap-
door, and when this is removed a step-ladder may
be seen leading down into the recess.[1]   The other

---

[1] The hiding-place in the garret measures about 5 feet 2 inches
in depth by $3\frac{1}{2}$ or $4\frac{1}{2}$ feet in width.

place behind the wainscot is situated in a chimney stack and is more roomy in its proportions. Here again is an inner hiding-place, entered through a trap-door in the floor, with a narrow staircase leading to an exit in the basement. So much for Boscobel.

Moseley Hall is thus referred to by the King : "I . . . sent Penderell's brother to Mr. Pitchcroft's [Whitgreaves] to know whether my Lord Wilmot was there or no, and had word brought me by him at night that my lord was there, that there was a *very secure hiding-hole* in Mr. Pitchcroft's house, and that he desired me to come thither to him."

It was while at Moseley the King had a very narrow escape. A search-party arrived on the scene and demanded admittance. Charles's host himself gives the account of this adventure : " In the afternoon [the King] reposing himself on his bed in the parlour chamber and inclineing to sleep, as I was watching at the window, one of the neighbours

I saw come running in, who told the maid soldiers were comeing to search, who thereupon presentlie came running to the staires head, and cried, 'Soldiers, soldiers are coming,' which his majestie hearing presentlie started out of his bedd and run to *his privacie, where I secured him the best I could,* and then leaving him, went forth into the street to meet the soldiers who were comeing to search, who as soon as they saw and knew who I was were readie to pull mee to pieces, and take me away with them, saying I was come from the Worcester fight ; but after much dispute with them, and by the neighbours being informed of their false information that I was not there, being very ill a great while, they let mee goe ; but till I saw them clearly all gone forth of the town I returned not ; but as soon as they were, I returned to release him and did acquaint him with my stay, which hee thought long, and then hee began to bee very chearful again.

"In the interim, whilst I was disputing with the

INTERIOR OF "PRIEST'S HOLE," MOSELEY HALL, WORCESTERSHIRE.

soldiers, one of them called Southall came in the ffould and asked a smith, as hee was shooing horses there, if he could tell where the King was, and he should have a thousand pounds for his payns. . . . This Southall was a great priest-catcher."

The hiding-place is located beneath the floor of a cupboard, adjoining the quaint old panelled bedroom the King occupied while he was at Moseley. Even "the merry monarch" must have felt depressed in such a dismal hole as this, and we can picture his anxious expression, as he sat upon the rude seat of brick which occupies one end of it, awaiting the result of the sudden alarm. The cupboard orginally was screened with wainscoting, a panel of which could be opened and closed by a spring. Family tradition also says there was a outlet from the hiding-place in a brew-house chimney. Situated in a gable end of the building, near the old chapel, in a garret, there is another "priest's hole" large enough

only to admit of a person lying down full
length.

Before the old seat of the Whitgreaves was
restored some fifteen or twenty years ago it was
one of the most picturesque half-timber houses,
not only in Staffordshire, but in England. It
had remained practically untouched since the day
above alluded to (September 9th, 1651).

Before reaching Trent, in Somersetshire, the
much sought-for king had many hardships to
undergo and many strange experiences. We must,
however, confine our remarks to those of the old
buildings which offered him an asylum that could
boast a hiding-place.

Trent House was one of these. The very fact
that it originally belonged to the recusant Gerard
family is sufficient evidence. From the Gerards it
passed by marriage to the Wyndhams, who were
in residence in the year we speak of. That his
Majesty spent much of his time in the actual
hiding-place at Trent is very doubtful. Alto-

gether he was safely housed here for over a fortnight, and during that time doubtless occasional
alarms drove him, as at Moseley, into his sanctuary; but a secluded room was set apart for his
use, where he had ample space to move about,
and from which he could reach his hiding-place at
a moment's notice. The black oak panelling and
beams of this cosy apartment, with its deep window
recesses, readily carries the mind back to the
time when its royal inmate wiled away the
weary hours by cooking his meals and amusing
himself as best he could—indeed a hardship for
one, such as he, so fond of outdoor exercise.

Close to the fireplace are two small, square,
secret panels, at one time used for the secretion
of sacred books or vessels, valuables or compromising deeds, but pointed out to visitors as a
kind of buttery hatch through which Charles II.
received his food. The King by day, also
according to local tradition, is said to have kept
up communication with his friends in the house

7

by means of a string suspended in the kitchen
chimney. That apartment is immediately beneath,
and has a fireplace of huge dimensions. An
old Tudor doorway leading into this part of
the house is said to have been screened from
observation by a load of hay.

Now for the hiding-place. Between this and
" my Lady Wyndham's chamber " (the aforesaid
panelled room that was kept exclusively for Charles's
use) was a small ante-room, long since demolished,
its position being now occupied by a rudely constructed staircase, from the landing of which the
hiding-place is now entered. The small secret
apartment is approached through a triangular hole
in the wall, something after the fashion of that
at Ufton Court ; but when one has squeezed
through this aperture he will find plenty of room
to stretch his limbs. The hole, which close
up against the rafters of the roof of the staircase
landing, when viewed from the inside of the apartment, is situated at the base of a blocked-up

stone Tudor doorway. Beneath the boards of the floor—as at Boscobel and Moseley—is an inner hiding-place, from which it was formerly possible to find an exit through the brew-house chimney.

It was from Trent House that Charles visited the Dorsetshire coast in the hopes of getting clear of England ; but a complication of misadventures induced him to hasten back with all speed to the pretty little village of Trent, to seek once more shelter beneath the roof of the Royalist Colonel Wyndham.

To resume the King's account :—

" As soon as we came to Frank Windham's I sent away presently to Colonel Robert Philips [Phelips], who lived then at Salisbury, to see what he could do for the getting me a ship ; which he undertook very willingly, and had got one at Southampton, but by misfortune she was amongst others prest to transport their soldiers to Jersey, by which she failed us also.

"Upon this, I sent further into Sussex, where Robin Philips knew one Colonel Gunter, to see whether he could hire a ship anywhere upon that coast. And not thinking it convenient for me to stay much longer at Frank Windham's (where I had been in all about a fortnight, and was become known to very many), I went directly away to a widow gentlewoman's house, one Mrs. Hyde, some four or five miles from Salisbury, where I came into the house just as it was almost dark, with Robin Philips only, not intending at first to make myself known. But just as I alighted at the door, Mrs. Hyde knew me, though she had never seen me but once in her life, and that was with the king, my father, in the army, when we marched by Salisbury some years before, in the time of the war; but she, being a discreet woman, took no notice at that time of me, I passing only for a friend of Robin Philips', by whose advice I went thither.

"At supper there was with us Frederick Hyde,

since a judge, and his sister-in-law, a widow,
Robin Philips, myself, and Dr. Henshaw [Hench-
man], since Bishop of London, whom I had
appointed to meet me there.

" While we were at supper, I observed Mrs.
Hyde and her brother Frederick to look a little
earnestly at me, which led me to believe they
might know me.   But I was not at all startled
by it, it having been my purpose to let her
know who I was ; and, accordingly, after supper
Mrs. Hyde came to me, and I discovered myself
to her, who told me she had a very safe place
to hide me in, till we knew whether our ship
was ready or no.   But she said it was not safe
for her to trust anybody but herself and her
sister, and therefore advised me to take my horse
next morning and make as if I quitted the house,
and return again about night ; for she would
order it so that all her servants and everybody
should be out of the house but herself and her
sister, whose name I remember not.

" So Robin Philips and I took our horses and went as far as Stonehenge ; and there we staid looking upon the stones for some time, and returned back again to Hale [Heale] (the place where Mrs. Hyde lived) about the hour she appointed ; where I went up into the hiding-hole, that was very convenient and safe, and staid there all alone (Robin Philips then going away to Salisbury) some four or five days."

Both exterior and interior of Heale House as it stands to-day point to a later date than 1651, though there are here and there vestiges of architecture anterior to the middle of the seventeenth century ; the hiding-place, however, is not among these, and looks nothing beyond a very deep cupboard adjoining one of the bedrooms, with nothing peculiar to distinguish it from ordinary cupboards.

But for all its modern innovations there is something about Heale which suggests a house with a history. Whether it is its environment of winding river and ancient cedar-trees, its venerable stables and imposing entrance gate, or the fact that it is one of those distinguished houses that have saved the life of an English king, we will not undertake to fathom.

CHAPTER VIII

CAVALIER-HUNTING, ETC.

A N old mansion in the precincts of the cathedral at Salisbury is said to have been a favourite hiding-place for fugitive cavaliers at the time of the Civil War. There is an inn immediately opposite this house, just outside the close, where the landlord (formerly a servant to the family who lived in the mansion) during the troublous times acted as a secret agent for those who were concealed, and proved invaluable by conveying messages and in other ways aiding those Royalists whose lives were in danger.

There are still certain " priests' holes " in the house, but the most interesting hiding-place is situated in the most innocent-looking of summer-

SECRET PANEL IN THE SALISBURY SUMMER-HOUSE.

houses in the grounds. The interior of this little
structure is wainscoted round with large panels,
like most of the summer-houses, pavilions, or
music-rooms of the seventeenth century, and
nothing uncommon or mysterious was discovered
until some twenty-five years ago. By the merest
accident one of the panels was found to open,
revealing what appeared to be an ordinary
cupboard with shelves. Further investigations,
however, proved its real object. By sliding one
of the shelves out of the grooves into which
it is fixed, a very narrow, disguised door, a
little over a foot in width, in the side of the
cupboard and in the thickness of the wall can
be opened. This again reveals a narrow passage,
or staircase, leading up to the joists above the
ceiling, and thence to a recess situated immediately
behind the carved ornamental facing over the
entrance door of the summer-house. In this
there is a narrow chink or peep-hole, from which
the fugitive could keep on the look-out either

for danger or for the friendly Royalist agent
of the " King's Arms."

When it was first discovered there were
evidences of its last occupant—*viz.* a Jacobean
horn tumbler, a mattress, and a handsomely
worked velvet pillow ; the last two articles,
provided no doubt for the comfort of some
hunted cavalier, upon being handled, fell to
pieces. It may be mentioned that the inner
door of the cupboard can be securely fastened
from the inside by an iron hook and staple for
that purpose.

Hewitt, mine host of the " King's Arms," was
not idle at the time transactions were in progress
to transfer Charles II. from Trent to Heale, and
received within his house Lord Wilmot, Colonel
Phelips, and other of the King's friends who
were actively engaged in making preparations
for the memorable journey. This old inn, with
its oak-panelled rooms and rambling corridors,
makes a very suitable neighbour to the more

SECRET CHAMBER AT CHASTLETON, OXFORDSHIRE.

dignified old brick mansion opposite, with which it is so closely associated.

Many are the exciting stories related of the defeated Royalists, especially after the Worcester fight. One of them, Lord Talbot, hastened to his paternal home of Longford, near Newport (Salop), and had just time to conceal himself ere his pursuers arrived, who, finding his horse saddled, concluded that the rider could not be far off. They therefore searched the house minutely for four or five days, and the fugitive would have perished for want of food, had not one of the servants contrived, at great personal risk, to pay him nocturnal visits and supply him with nourishment.

The grey old Jacobean mansion Chastleton preserves in its oak-panelled hall the sword and portrait of the gallant cavalier Captain Arthur Jones, who, narrowly escaping from the battlefield, speeded homewards with some of Cromwell's soldiers at his heels ; and his wife, a lady of great courage, had scarcely concealed him in the secret chamber when the enemy arrived to search the house.

Little daunted, the lady, with great presence of mind, made no objection whatever—indeed, facilitated their operations by personally conducting them over the mansion. Here, as in so many other instances, the secret room was entered from the principal bedroom, and in inspecting the latter the suspicion of the Roundheads was in some way or another aroused, so here they determined to remain for the rest of the night.

An ample supper and a good store of wine (which, by the way, had been carefully drugged) was sent up to the unwelcome visitors, and in due course the drink effected its purpose—its victims dropped off one by one, until the whole party lay like logs upon the floor. Mrs. Arthur Jones then crept in, having even to step over the bodies of the inanimate Roundheads, released her

husband, and a fresh horse being in readiness,
by the time the effects of the wine had worn
off the Royalist captain was far beyond their
reach.

The secret room is located in the front of the
building, and has now been converted into a very
comfortable little dressing-room, preserving its
original oak panelling, and otherwise but little
altered, with the exception of the entry to it,
which is now an ordinary door.

Chastleton is the beau ideal of an ancestral hall.
The grand old gabled house, with its lofty square
towers, its Jacobean entrance gateway and dove-
cote, and the fantastically clipped box-trees and
sun-dial of its quaint old-fashioned garden, possesses
a charm which few other ancient mansions can
boast, and this charm lies in its perfectly unaltered
state throughout, even to the minutest detail.
Interior and exterior alike, everything presents an
appearance exactly as it did when it was erected
and furnished by Walter Jones, Esquire, between

the years 1603 and 1630. The estate originally
was held by Robert Catesby, who sold the house
to provide funds for carrying on the notorious
conspiracy, since which time it has remained in
the hands of the Jones family.

Among its most valued relics is a Bible
given by Charles I. when on the scaffold to
Bishop Juxon, who lived at Little Compton
manor house, near Chastleton. This Bible was
always used by the bishop at the Divine
services, which at one time were held in the
great hall of the latter house. Other relics of
the martyr-king used to be at Little Compton—
viz. some beams of the Whitehall scaffold, whose
exact position has occasioned so much controversy.
The velvet armchair and footstool used by the
King during his memorable trial were also preserved here, but of late years have found a home
at Moreton-in-the-Marsh, some six miles away.
Visitors to that interesting collection shown in
London some years ago—the Stuart Exhibition—

CHASTLETON, OXFORDSHIRE.

may remember this venerable armchair of such sad association.

It may be here stated that after Charles I.'s execution, Juxon lived for a time in Sussex at an old mansion still extant, Albourne Place, not far from Hurstpierpoint. We mention this from the fact that a priest's hole was discovered there some few years ago. It was found in opening a communication between two rooms, and originally it could only be reached by steps projecting from the inner walls of a chimney.

Not many miles from Albourne stands Street Place, an Elizabethan Sussex house of some note. A remarkable story of cavalier-hunting is told here. A hiding-place is said to have existed in the wide open fireplace of the great hall. Tradition has it that a horseman, hard pressed by the Parliamentary troopers, galloped into this hall, but upon the arrival of his pursuers, no clue could be found of either man or horse!

The gallant Prince Rupert himself, upon one

occasion, is said to have had recourse to a hiding-hole, at least so the story runs, at the beautiful old black-and-white timber mansion, Park Hall, near Oswestry. A certain "false floor" which led to it is pointed out in a cupboard of a bedroom, the hiding-place itself being situated immediately above the dining-room fireplace.

A concealed chamber something after the same description is to be seen at the old seat of the Fenwicks, Wallington, in Northumberland—a small room eight feet long by sixteen feet high, situated at the back of the dining-room fireplace, and approached through the back of a cupboard.

Behind one of the large panels of "the hall" of an old building in Warwick called St. John's Hospital is a hiding-place, and in a bedroom of the same house there is a little apartment, now converted into a dressing-room, which formerly could only be reached through a sliding panel over the fireplace.

The manor house of Dinsdale-on-Tees, Durham,

BROUGHTON HALL, STAFFORDSHIRE.

ST. JOHN'S HOSPITAL, WARWICK.

has another example, but to reach it it is necessary to pass through a trap-door in the attics, crawl along under the roof, and drop down into the space in the wall behind a bedroom fireplace, where for extra security there is a second trap-door.

Full-length panel portraits of the Salwey family at Stanford Court, Worcestershire (unfortunately burned down in 1882), concealed hidden recesses and screened passages leading up to an exit in the leads of the roof. In one of these recesses curious seventeenth-century manuscripts were found, among them, the household book of a certain " Joyce Jeffereys " during the Civil War.

The old Jacobean mansion Broughton Hall, Staffordshire, had a curious hiding-hole over a fireplace and situated in the wall between the dining-room and the great hall ; over its entrance used to hang a portrait of a man in antique costume which went by the name of " Red Stockings."

At Lyme Hall, Cheshire, the ancient seat of

the Leghs, high up in the wall of the hall is a
sombre portrait which by ingenious mechanism
swings out of its frame, a fixture, and gives
admittance to a room on the first floor, or rather
affords a means of looking down into the hall.[1]
We mention this portrait more especially because
it has been supposed that Scott got his idea here
of the ghostly picture which figures in *Woodstock*.
A *bonâ-fide* hiding-place, however, is to be seen in
another part of the mansion in a very haunted-
looking bedroom called "the Knight's Chamber,"
entered through a trap-door in the floor of a
cupboard, with a short flight of steps leading
into it.

Referring to Scott's novel, a word may be said
about Fair Rosamond's famous "bower" at the
old palace of Woodstock, surely the most elaborate
and complicated hiding-place ever devised.   The

---

[1] A large panel in the long gallery of Hatfield can be pushed
aside, giving a view into the great hall, and at Ockwells and
other ancient mansions this device may also be seen.

STAIRCASE, BROUGHTON HALL.

ruins of the labyrinth leading to the "bower" existed in Drayton's time, who described them as "vaults, arched and walled with stone and brick, almost inextricably wound within one another, by which, if at any time her [Rosamond's] lodging were laid about by the Queen, she might easily avoid peril imminent, and, if need be, by secret issues take the air abroad many furlongs about Woodstock."

In a survey taken in 1660, it is stated that foundation signs remained about a bow-shot south-west of the gate : "*The form and circuit both of the place and ruins show it to have been a house of one pile, and probably was filled with secret places of recess and avenues to hide or convey away such persons as were not willing to be found if narrowly sought after.*"

Ghostly gambols, such as those actually practised upon the Parliamentary Commissioners at the old palace of Woodstock, were for years carried on without detection by the servants at the old house

of Hinton-Ampner, Hampshire ; and when it was
pulled down in the year 1797, it became very
obvious how the mysteries, which gave the house
the reputation of being haunted, were managed,
for numerous secret stairs and passages, not known
to exist were brought to light which had offered
peculiar facilities for the deception.   About the
middle of the eighteenth century the mansion
passed out of the hands of its old possessors, the
Stewkeleys, and shortly afterwards became notorious
for the unaccountable noises which disturbed the
peace of mind of the new tenants.   Not only were
there violent knocks, hammerings, groanings, and
sounds of footsteps in the ceilings and walls, but
strange sights frightened the servants out of their
wits.   A ghostly visitant dressed in drab would
appear   and   disappear   mysteriously,   a   female
figure was often seen to rush through the apartments,   and   other   supernatural   occurrences   at
length became so intolerable that the inmates of
the house sought refuge in flight.   Later successive

tenants fared the same. A hundred pounds reward was offered to any who should run the ghosts to earth ; but nothing resulted from it, and after thirty years or more of hauntings, the house was razed to the ground. Secret passages and chambers were then brought to light ; but those who had carried on the deception for so long took the secret with them to their graves.[1]

It is well known that the huge, carved oak bedsteads of the sixteenth and seventeenth centuries were often provided with secret accommodation for valuables. One particular instance we can call to mind of a hidden cupboard at the base of the bedpost which contained a short rapier. But of these small hiding-places we shall speak presently. It is with the head of the bed we have now to do, as it was sometimes used as an opening into the wall at the back. Occasionally, in old houses, unmeaning gaps and spaces are

---

[1] A full account of the supernatural occurrences at Hinton-Ampner will be found in the Life of Richard Barham.

met with in the upper rooms midway between floor and ceiling, which possibly at one time were used as bed-head hiding-places. Shipton Court, Oxon, and Hill Hall, Essex, may be given as examples. Dunster Castle, Somersetshire, also, has at the back of a bedstead in one of the rooms a long, narrow place of concealment, extending the width of the apartment, and provided with a stone seat.

Sir Ralph Verney, while in exile in France in 1645, wrote to his brother at Claydon House, Buckinghamshire, concerning "the odd things in the room my mother kept herself—*the iron chest in the little room between her bed's-head and the back stairs.*" This old seat of the Verneys had another secret chamber in the middle storey, entered through a trap-door in "the muniment-room" at the top of the house. Here also was a small private staircase in the wall, possibly the " back stairs " mentioned in Sir Ralph's letters.[1]

[1] See *Memoirs of the Verney Family.*

SHIPTON COURT, OXFORDSHIRE.

Before the breaking out of the Civil War,
Hampden, Pym, Lord Brooke, and other of
the Parliamentary leaders, held secret meetings
at Broughton Castle, Oxon, the seat of Lord Saye
and Sele, to organise a resistance to the arbitrary
measures of the king. In this beautiful old
fortified and moated mansion the secret stairs may
yet be seen that led up to the little isolated
chamber, with massive casemated walls for the
exclusion of sound. Anthony Wood, alluding
to the secret councils, says : " Several years before
the Civil War began, Lord Saye, being looked
upon as the godfather of that party, had meetings
of them in his house at Broughton, where was
a room and passage thereunto which his servants
were prohibited to come near." [1] There is also
a hiding-hole behind a window shutter in the
wall of a corridor, with an air-hole ingeniously
devised in the masonry.

The old dower-house of Fawsley, not many

[1] *Memorials of Hampden.*

miles to the north-east of Broughton, in the adjoining county of Northamptonshire, had a secret room over the hall, where a private press was kept for the purpose of printing political tracts at this time, when the country was working up into a state of turmoil.

When the regicides were being hunted out in the early part of Charles II.'s reign, Judge Mayne [1] secreted himself at his house, Dinton Hall, Bucks, but eventually gave himself up. The hiding-hole at Dinton was beneath the staircase, and accessible by removing three of the steps. A narrow passage which led from it to a space behind the beams of the roof had its sides or walls thickly lined with cloth, so as to muffle all sound.

Bradshawe Hall, in north-west Derbyshire, once the seat of President Bradshawe, has or had a concealed chamber high up in the wall of a room on the ground floor which was capable of

[1] There is a tradition that it was a servant of Mayne who acted as Charles I.'s executioner.

ENTRANCE GATE, BRADSHAWE HALL, DERBYSHIRE.

holding three persons. Of course tradition says the "wicked judge was hidden here."

The regicides Colonels Whalley and Goffe had many narrow escapes in America, whither they were traced. What is known as "Judge's Cave," in the West Rock some two miles from the town of New Haven, Conn., afforded them sanctuary. For some days they were concealed in an old house belonging to a certain Mrs. Eyers, in a secret chamber behind the wainscoting, the entrance to which was most ingeniously devised. The house was narrowly searched on May 14th, 1661, at the time they were in hiding.[1]

Upon the discovery of the Rye House Plot in 1683, suspicion falling upon one of the conspirators, William, third Lord Howard of Escrick, the Sergeant-at-Arms was despatched with a squadron of horse to his house at Knightsbridge, and after a long search he was discovered concealed in a hiding-place constructed in a

[1] Stiles's *Judges*, p. 64.

chimney at the back of a tall cupboard, and the
chances are that he would not have been arrested
had it not been evident, by the warmth of his
bed and his clothes scattered about, that he had
only just risen and could not have got away
unobserved, except to some concealed lurking-
place. When discovered he had on no clothing
beyond his shirt, so it may be imagined with
what precipitate haste he had to hide himself upon
the unexpected arrival of the soldiers.[1]

Numerous other houses were searched for arms
and suspicious papers, particularly in the counties
of Cheshire and Lancashire, where the Duke of
Monmouth was known to have many influential
friends, marked enemies to the throne.[2]

Monmouth's lurking-place was known at Whitehall, and those who revealed it went the wrong
way to work to win Court favour. Apart from
the attractions of Lady Wentworth, whose com-

---

[1] See Roger North's *Examen.*
[2] See Oulton Hall MSS., Hist. MSS. Com. Rep. iii. p. 245.

MOYLES COURT, HAMPSHIRE.

panionship made the fugitive's enforced seclusion at Toddington, in Bedfordshire, far from tedious, the mansion was desirable at that particular time on account of its hiding facilities. An anonymous letter sent to the Secretary of State failed not to point out "that vastness and intricacy that without a most diligent search it's impossible to discover *all the lurking holes in it, there being severall trap dores on the leads and in closetts, into places to which there is no other access.*" [1] The easy-going king had to make some external show towards an attempt to capture his erring son, therefore instructions were given with this purpose, but to a courtier and diplomatist who valued his own interests. Toddington Place, therefore, was *not* explored.

Few hiding-places are associated with so tragic a story as that at Moyles Court, Hants, where the venerable Lady Alice Lisle, in pure charity, hid two partisans of Monmouth, John Hickes

[1] Vide *King Monmouth.*

and Richard Nelthorpe, after the battle of
Sedgemoor, for which humane action she was
condemned to be burned alive by Judge Jeffreys
—a sentence commuted afterwards to beheading.
It is difficult to associate this peaceful old
Jacobean mansion, and the simple tomb in the
churchyard hard by, with so terrible a history.
A dark hole in the wall of the kitchen is
traditionally said to be the place of concealment
of the fugitives, who threw themselves on Lady
Alice's mercy ; but a dungeon-like cellar not
unlike that represented in E. M. Ward's well-
known picture looks a much more likely place.

It was in an underground vault at Lady Place,
Hurley, the old seat of the Lovelaces, that secret
conferences were held by the adherents of the
Prince of Orange. Three years after the execution
of the Duke of Monmouth, his boon companion
and supporter, John, third Lord Lovelace, organised
treasonable meetings in this tomb-like chamber.
Tradition asserts that certain important documents

in favour of the Revolution were actually signed in the Hurley vault. Be this as it may, King William III. failed not, in after years, when visiting his former secret agent, to inspect the subterranean apartment with very tender regard.

CHAPTER IX

JAMES II.'S ESCAPES

WE have spoken of the old houses associated
with Charles II.'s escapes, let us see what
history has to record of his unpopular brother
James. The Stuarts seem to have been doomed,
at one time or another, to evade their enemies
by secret flight, and in some measure this may
account for the romance always surrounding that
ill-fated line of kings and queens.

James V. of Scotland was wont to amuse himself
by donning a disguise, but his successors appear
to have been doomed by fate to follow his
example, not for recreation, but to preserve their
lives.

Mary, Queen of Scots, upon one occasion had

to impersonate a laundress. Her grandson and great-grandson both were forced to masquerade as servants, and her great-great-grandson Prince James Frederick Edward passed through France disguised as an abbé.

The escapades of his son the "Bonnie Prince" will require our attention presently ; we will, therefore, for the moment confine our thoughts to James II.

With the surrender of Oxford the young Prince James found himself Fairfax's prisoner. His elder brother Charles had been more fortunate, having left the city shortly before for the western counties, and after effecting his escape to Scilly, he sought refuge in Jersey, whence he removed to the Hague. The Duke of Gloucester and the Princess Elizabeth already had been placed under the custody of the Earl of Northumberland at St. James's Palace, so the Duke of York was sent there also. This was in 1646. Some nine months elapsed, and James, after two ineffectual attempts to regain his liberty, eventually succeeded in the following manner.

Though prisoners, the royal children were permitted to amuse themselves within the walls of the palace much as they pleased, and among the juvenile games with which they passed away the time, " hide-and-seek " was first favourite. James, doubtless with an eye to the future, soon acquired a reputation as an expert hider, and his brother and sister and the playmates with whom they associated would frequently search the odd nooks and corners of the old mansion in vain for an hour at a stretch. It was, therefore, no extraordinary occurrence on the night of April 20th, 1647, that the Prince, after a prolonged search, was missing. The youngsters, more than usually perplexed, presently persuaded the adults of the prison establishment to join in the game, which, when their suspicions were aroused, they did in real earnest. But all in vain, and at length a messenger was despatched to Whitehall with the intelligence that James, Duke of York, had effected his escape. Everything was in a turmoil. Orders were hurriedly dispatched for all seaport towns to be on the alert, and every exit out of London was strictly watched ; meanwhile, it is scarcely necessary to add, the young fugitive was well clear of the city, speeding on his way to the Continent.

The plot had been skilfully planned. A key, or rather a duplicate key, had given admittance through the gardens into St. James's Park, where the Royalist, though outwardly professed Parliamentarian, Colonel Bamfield was in readiness with a periwig and cloak to effect a speedy disguise. When at length the fugitive made his appearance, minus his shoes and coat, he was hurried into a coach and conveyed to the Strand by Salisbury House, where the two alighted, and passing down Ivy Lane, reached the river, and after James's disguise had been perfected, boat was taken to Lyon Quay in Lower Thames Street, where a barge lay in readiness to carry them down stream.

So far all went well, but on the way to Gravesend

9

the master of the vessel, doubtless with a view to increasing his reward, raised some objections. The fugitive was now in female attire, and the objection was that nothing had been said about a woman coming aboard ; but he was at length pacified, indeed ere long guessed the truth, for the Prince's lack of female decorum, as in the case of his grandson " the Bonnie Prince " nearly a century afterwards, made him guess how matters really stood. Beyond Gravesend the fugitives got aboard a Dutch vessel and were carried safely to Middleburg.

We will now shift the scene to Whitehall in the year 1688, when, after a brief reign of three years, betrayed and deserted on all sides, the unhappy Stuart king was contemplating his second flight out of England. The weather-cock that had been set up on the banqueting hall to show when the wind " blew Protestant " had duly recorded the dreaded approach of Dutch William, who now was steadily advancing towards the capital.

On Tuesday, December 10th, soon after midnight, James left the Palace by way of Chiffinch's secret stairs of notorious fame, and disguised as the servant of Sir Edward Hales, with Ralph Sheldon— La Badie—a page, and Dick Smith, a groom, attending him, crossed the river to Lambeth, dropping the great seal in the water on the way, and took horse, avoiding the main roads, towards Farnborough and thence to Chislehurst. Leaving Maidstone to the south-west, a brief halt was made at Pennenden Heath for refreshment. The old inn, " the Woolpack," where the party stopped for their hurried repast, remains, at least in name, for the building itself has of late years been replaced by a modern structure. Crossing the Dover road, the party now directed their course towards Milton Creek, to the north-east of Sittingbourne, where a small fishing-craft lay in readiness, which had been chartered by Sir Edward Hales, whose seat at Tunstall[1] was close by.

[1] The principal seat of the Hales, near Canterbury, is now

One or two old buildings in the desolate marsh
district of Elmley, claim the distinction of having
received a visit of the deposed monarch prior to
the mishaps which were shortly to follow. King's
Hill Farm, once a house of some importance,
preserves this tradition, as does also an ancient
cottage, in the last stage of decay, known as
" Rats' Castle."

At Elmley Ferry, which crosses the river
Swale, the king got aboard, but scarcely had
the moorings been cast than further progress
was arrested by a party of over-zealous fishermen
on the look out for fugitive Jesuit priests. The
story of the rough handling to which the poor
king was subjected is a somewhat hackneyed
school-book anecdote, but some interesting details
have been handed down by one Captain Marsh,

occupied as a Jesuit College. The old manor house of Tunstall,
Grove End Farm, presents both externally and internally many
features of interest. The family was last represented by a maiden
lady who died a few years since.

KING'S HILL FARM, ELMLEY, KENT.

by James's natural son the Duke of Berwick, and
by the Earl of Ailesbury.

From these accounts we gather that in the dis-
turbance that ensued a blow was aimed at the King,
but that a Canterbury innkeeper named Platt threw
himself in the way and received the blow himself.
It is recorded, to James II.'s credit, that when he
was recognised and his stolen money and jewels
offered back to him, he declined the former,
desiring that his health might be drunk by the
mob.   Among the valuables were the King's
watch, his coronation ring, and medals commemor-
ating the births of his son the Chevalier St. George
and of his brother Charles II.

The King was taken ashore at a spot called "the
Stool," close to the little village of Oare, to the
north-west of Faversham, to which town he was
conveyed by coach, attended by a score of Kentish
gentlemen on horseback.   The royal prisoner was
first carried to the "Queen's Arms Inn," which
still exists under the name of the "Ship Hotel."

From here he was taken to the mayor's house in Court Street (an old building recently pulled down to make way for a new brewery) and placed under a strict guard, and from the window of his prison the unfortunate King had to listen to the proclamation of the Prince of Orange, read by order of the mayor, who subsequently was rewarded for the zeal he displayed upon the occasion.

The hardships of the last twenty-four hours had told severely upon James. He was sick and feeble and weakened by profuse bleeding of the nose, to which he, like his brother Charles, was subject when unduly excited. Sir Edward Hales, in the meantime, was lodged in the old Court Hall (since partially rebuilt), whence he was removed to Maidstone gaol, and to the Tower.

Bishop Burnet was at Windsor with the Prince of Orange when two gentlemen arrived there from Faversham with the news of the King's capture. "They told me," he says, " of the accident at Faversham, and desired to know the Prince's pleasure. upon it. I was affected with this dismal reverse of the fortunes of a great prince, more than I think fit to express. I went immediately to Bentinck and wakened him, and got him to go in to the Prince, and let him know what had happened, that some order might be presently given for the security of the King's person, and for taking him out of the hands of a rude multitude who said they would obey no orders but such as came from the Prince."

Upon receiving the news, William at once directed that his father-in-law should have his liberty, and that assistance should be sent down to him immediately ; but by this time the story had reached the metropolis, and a hurried meeting of the Council directed the Earl of Feversham to go to the rescue with a company of Life Guards. The faithful Earl of Ailesbury also hastened to the King's assistance. In five hours he accomplished the journey from London to Faversham. So rapidly had the reports been circulated of

supposed ravages of the Irish Papists, that when
the Earl reached Rochester, the entire town was
in a state of panic, and the alarmed inhabitants
were busily engaged in demolishing the bridge to
prevent the dreaded incursion.

But to return to James at Faversham. The
mariners who had handled him so roughly now
took his part—in addition to his property—
and insisted upon sleeping in the adjoining room
to that in which he was incarcerated, to protect
him from further harm. Early on Saturday
morning the Earl of Feversham made his
appearance ; and after some little hesitation on
the King's side, he was at length persuaded to
return to London. So he set out on horseback,
breaking the journey at Rochester, where he slept
on the Saturday night at Sir Richard Head's house.
On the Sunday he rode on to Dartford, where
he took coach to Southwark and Whitehall. A
temporary reaction had now set in, and the
cordial reception which greeted his reappearance

ENTRANCE TO SECRET PASSAGE, "ABDICATION HOUSE," ROCHESTER.

revived his hopes and spirits. This reaction, however, was but short-lived, for no sooner had the poor King retired to the privacy of his bed-chamber at Whitehall Palace, than an imperious message from his son-in-law ordered him to remove without delay to Ham House, Petersham.

James objected strongly to this ; the place, he said, was damp and unfurnished (which, by the way, was not the case if we may judge from Evelyn, who visited the mansion not long before, when it was "furnished like a great Prince's"—indeed, the same furniture remains intact to this day), and a message was sent back that if he must quit Whitehall he would prefer to retire to Rochester, which wish was readily accorded him.

CHAPTER X

JAMES II.'S ESCAPES (*continued*),
HAM HOUSE, AND "ABDICATION HOUSE"

TRADITION, regardless of fact, associates the grand old seat of the Lauderdales and Dysarts with King James's escape from England. A certain secret staircase is still pointed out by which the dethroned monarch is said to have made his exit, and visitors to the Stuart Exhibition a few years ago will remember a sword which, with the King's hat and cloak, is said to have been left behind when he quitted the mansion. Now there existed, not many miles away, also close to the river Thames, *another* Ham House, which was closely associated with James II., and it seems, therefore, possible, in fact probable, that

the past associations of the one house have attached themselves to the other.

In Ham House, Weybridge, lived for some years the King's discarded mistress Catherine Sedley, Countess of Dorchester. At the actual time of James's abdication this lady was in France, but in the earlier part of his reign the King was a frequent visitor here. In Charles II.'s time the house belonged to Jane Bickerton, the mistress and afterwards wife of the sixth Duke of Norfolk. Evelyn dined there soon after this marriage had been solemnised. " The Duke," he says, " leading me about the house made no scruple of showing me all the hiding-places for the Popish priests and where they said Masse, for he was no bigoted Papist." At the Duke's death " the palace " was sold to the Countess of Dorchester, whose descendants pulled it down some fifty years ago. The oak-panelled rooms were richly parquetted with " cedar and cyprus." One of them until the last retained the name of " the King's Bedroom."

It had a private communication with a little
Roman Catholic chapel in the building. The
attics, as at Compton Winyates, were called "the
Barracks," tradition associating them with the
King's guards, who are said to have been lodged
there. Upon the walls hung portraits of the
Duchesses of Leeds and Dorset, of Nell Gwyn
and the Countess herself, and of Earl Portmore,
who married her daughter. Here also formerly
was Holbein's famous picture, Bluff King Hal and
the Dukes of Suffolk and Norfolk dancing a
minuet with Anne Boleyn and the Dowager-
Queens of France and Scotland. Evelyn saw the
painting in August, 1678, and records "the
sprightly motion" and "amorous countenances
of the ladies." (This picture is now, or was
recently, in the possession of Major-General
Sotheby.)

A few years after James's abdication, the Earl of
Ailesbury rented the house from the Countess, who
lived meanwhile in a small house adjacent, and

MONUMENT TO SIR RICHARD HEAD.

"RESTORATION HOUSE," ROCHESTER.

was in the habit of coming into the gardens of
the palace by a key of admittance she kept for
that purpose.   Upon one of these occasions the Earl
and she had a disagreement about the lease, and
so forcible were the lady's coarse expressions, for
she never could restrain the licence of her tongue,
that she had to be ejected from the premises,
whereupon, says Ailesbury, "she bade me go to
my —— King James," with the assurance that
"she would make King William spit on me."

But to follow James II.'s ill-fortunes to Rochester,
where he was conveyed on the Tuesday at noon
by royal barge, with an escort of Dutch soldiers,
with Lords Arran, Dumbarton, etc., in attendance—
"a sad sight," says Evelyn, who witnessed the
departure.   The King recognised among those
set to guard him an old lieutenant of the Horse
who had fought under him, when Duke of York,
at the battle of Dunkirk.   Colonel Wycke, in
command of the King's escort, was a nephew of
the court painter Sir Peter Lely, who had owed

his success to the patronage of Charles II. and his brother. The part the Colonel had to act was a painful one, and he begged the King's pardon. The royal prisoner was lodged for the night at Gravesend, at the house of a lawyer, and next morning the journey was continued to Rochester.

The royalist Sir Richard Head again had the honour of acting as the King's host, and his guest was allowed to go in and out of the house as he pleased, for diplomatic William of Orange had arranged that no opportunity should be lost for James to make use of a passport which the Duke of Berwick had obtained for " a certain gentleman and two servants." James's movements, therefore, were hampered in no way. But the King, ever suspicious, planned his escape from Rochester with the greatest caution and secrecy, and many of his most attached and loyal adherents were kept in ignorance of his final departure. James's little court consisted of the Earls of Arran, Lichfield, Middleton, Dumbarton, and Ailesbury, the Duke of

Berwick, Sir Stephen Fox, Major-General Sackville, Mr. Grahame, Fenton, and a few others.

On the evening of the King's flight the company dispersed as was customary, when Ailesbury intimated, by removing his Majesty's stockings, that the King was about to seek his couch. The Earl of Dumbarton retired with James to his apartment, who, when the house was quiet for the night, got up, dressed, and "by way of the back stairs," according to the Stuart Papers, passed "through the garden, where Macdonald stayed for him, with the Duke of Berwick and Mr. Biddulph, to show him the way to Trevanion's boat. About twelve at night they rowed down to the smack, which was waiting without the fort at Sheerness. It blew so hard right ahead, and ebb tide being done before they got to the Salt Pans, that it was near six before they got to the smack. Captain Trevanion not being able to trust the officers of his ship, they got on board the *Eagle* fireship, commanded by Captain Welford, on which, the wind and tide being against them, they stayed till daybreak, when the King went on board the smack." On Christmas Day James landed at Ambleteuse.

Thus the old town of Rochester witnessed the departure of the last male representative of the Stuart line who wore a crown. Twenty-eight years before, every window and gable end had been gaily bedecked with many coloured ribbons, banners, and flowers to welcome in the restored monarch. The picturesque old red brick " Restoration House" still stands to carry us back to the eventful night when " his sacred Majesty " slept within its walls upon his way from Dover to London—a striking contrast to " Abdication House," the gloomy abode of Sir Richard Head, of more melancholy associations.

Much altered and modernised, this old mansion also remains. It is in the High Street, and is now, or was recently, occupied as a draper's shop. Here may be seen the " presence-chamber " where the dethroned King heard Mass, and the royal bedchamber where, after his secret departure, a letter was found on the table addressed to Lord Middleton, for both he and Lord Ailesbury were kept in ignorance of James II.'s final movements. The old garden may be seen with the steps leading down to the river, much as it was a couple of centuries ago, though the river now no longer flows in near proximity, owing to the drainage of the marshes and the "subsequent improvements" of later days.

The hidden passage in the staircase wall may also be seen, and the trap-door leading to it from the attics above. Tradition says the King made use of these ; and if he did so, the probability is that it was done more to avoid his host's over-zealous neighbours, than from fear of arrest through the vigilance of the spies of his son-in-law.[1]

[1] It may be of interest to state that the illustrations we give of the house were originally exhibited at the Stuart Exhibition by Sir Robert G. Head, the living representative of the old Royalist family.

Exactly three months after James left England
he made his reappearance at Kinsale and entered
Dublin in triumphal state. The siege of
Londonderry and the decisive battle of the Boyne
followed, and for a third and last time James II.
was a fugitive from his realms. The melancholy
story is graphically told in Mr. A. C. Gow's
dramatic picture, an engraving of which I understand has recently been published.

How the unfortunate King rode from Dublin
to Duncannon Fort, leaving his faithful followers
and ill-fortunes behind him; got aboard the French
vessel anchored there for his safety; and returned
once more to the protection of the Grande
Monarque at the palace of St. Germain, is an
oft-told story of Stuart ingratitude.

CHAPTER XI

MYSTERIOUS ROOMS, DEADLY PITS, ETC.

AT the " Restoration House " previously mentioned there is a secret passage in the wall
of an upper room ; but though the Merry Monarch
is, according to popular tradition, credited with a
monopoly of hiding-places all over England,
it is more than doubtful whether he had recourse
to these exploits, in which he was so successful
in 1651, upon such a joyful occasion, except,
indeed, through sheer force of habit.

Even Cromwell's name is connected with hiding-
places ! But it is difficult to conjecture upon
what occasions his Excellency found it convenient
to secrete himself, unless it was in his later days,
when he went about in fear of assassination.

Hale House, Islington, pulled down in 1853, had a concealed recess behind the wainscot over the mantel-piece, formed by the curve of the chimney. In this, tradition says, the Lord Protector was hidden. Nor is this the solitary instance, for a dark hole in one of the gable ends of Cromwell House, Mortlake (taken down in 1860), locally known as " Old Noll's Hole," is said to have afforded him temporary accommodation when his was life in danger.[1] The residence of his son-in-law Ireton (Cromwell House) at Highgate contained a large secret chamber at the back of a cupboard in one of the upper rooms, and extended back twelve or fourteen feet, but the cupboard has now been removed and the space at the back converted into a passage.

The ancient manor house of Armscot, in an old-world corner of Worcestershire, contains in one of its gables a hiding-place entered through a narrow opening in the plaster wall, not unlike that at Ufton Court, and capable of holding many

[1] See Faulkner's *History of Islington.*

ARMSCOT MANOR HOUSE, WORCESTERSHIRE.

people. From the fact that George Fox was arrested in this house on October 17th, 1673, when he was being persecuted by the county magistrates, the story has come down to the yokels of the neighbourhood that " old Guy Fawkes, the first Quaker," was hidden here ! In his journal Fox mentions his arrest at Armscot after a "very large and precious meeting " in the barn close by ; but we have no allusion to the hiding-place, for he appears to have been sitting in the parlour when Henry Parker, the Justice, arrived—indeed, George Fox was not the sort of man to have recourse to concealments, and owe his escape to a " priest's hole."

The suggestion of a sudden reverse in religious persecution driving a Quaker to such an extremity calls to mind an old farmstead where a political change from monarchy to commonwealth forced Puritan and cavalier consecutively to seek refuge in the secret chamber. This narrow hiding-place, beside the spacious fire-place, is pointed out

in an ancient house in the parish of Hinchford,
in Eastern Essex.

Even the notorious Judge Jeffreys had in his
house facilities for concealment and escape. His
old residence in Delahay Street, Westminster,
demolished a few years ago, had its secret panel
in the wainscoting, but in what way the cruel Lord
Chancellor made use of it does not transpire;
possibly it may have been utilised at the time
of James II.'s flight from Whitehall.

A remarkable discovery was made early in the
last century at the Elizabethan manor house of
Bourton-on-the-Water, Gloucestershire, only a portion of which remains incorporated in a modern
structure. Upon removing some of the wall-
paper of a passage on the second floor, the entrance
to a room hitherto unknown was laid bare. It
was a small apartment about eight feet square, and
presented the appearance as if some occupant had
just quitted it. A chair and a table within, each
bore evidence of the last inmate. Over the back

of the former hung a priest's black cassock, care-
lessly flung there a century or more ago, while
on the table stood an antique tea-pot, cup, and
silver spoon, the very tea leaves crumbled to dust
with age. On the same storey were two rooms
known as " the chapel " and the " priest's room,"
the names of which signify the former use of the
concealed apartment.

Sir Walter Scott records a curious " find," similar
in many respects to that at Bourton. In the
course of some structural alterations to an ancient
house near Edinburgh three unknown rooms were
brought to light, bearing testimony of their last
inmate. One of them had been occupied as a
bedroom. The clothing of the bed was dis-
arranged, as if it had been slept in only a few
hours previously, and close by was an antique
dressing-gown. How interesting it would be to
know some particulars of the sudden surprise
which evidently drove the owner of the garment
from his snug quarters—whether he effected

his escape, or whether he was captured! The walls of this buried chamber, if they could speak, had some curious story to relate.

Not many years ago the late squire of East Hendred House, Berkshire, discovered the existence of a secret chamber in casually glancing over some ancient papers belonging to the house. " The little room," as it was called, from its proximity to the chapel, had no doubt been turned to good account during the penal laws of Elizabeth's reign, as the chamber itself and other parts of the house date from a much earlier period.

Long after the palatial Sussex mansion of Cowdray was burnt down, the habitable remains (the keeper's lodge, in the centre of the park) contained an ingenious hiding-place behind a fire-place in a bedroom, which was reached by a movable panel in a cupboard, communicating with the roof by a slender flight of steps. It was very high, reaching up two storeys, but extremely narrow, so much so that directly opposite a stone bench which stood in a recess for a seat, the wall was hollowed out to admit of the knees. When this secret chamber was discovered, it contained an iron chair, a quaint old brass lamp, and some manuscripts of the Montague family. The Cowdray tradition says that the fifth Viscount was concealed in this hiding-place for a considerable period, owing to some dark crime he is supposed to have committed, though he was generally believed to have fled abroad. Secret nocturnal interviews took place between Lord Montague and his wife in " My Lady's Walk," an isolated spot in Cowdray Park. The Montagues, now extinct, are said to have been very chary with reference to their Roman Catholic forefathers, and never allowed the secret chamber to be shown.[1]

A weird story clings to the ruins of Minster Lovel Manor House, Oxfordshire, the ancient seat of the Lords Lovel. After the battle of Stoke, Francis, the last Viscount, who had sided with the cause

[1] See *History of a Great English House.*

of Simnel against King Henry VII., fled back to
his house in disguise, but from the night of his
return was never seen or heard of again, and
for nearly two centuries his disappearance remained
a mystery. In the meantime the manor house
had been dismantled and the remains tenanted by
a farmer ; but a strange discovery was made in
the year 1708. A concealed vault was found,
and in it, seated before a table, with a prayer-
book lying open upon it, was the entire skeleton
of a man. In the secret chamber were certain
barrels and jars which had contained food sufficient
to last perhaps some weeks ; but the mansion having
been seized by the King, soon after the unfortunate
Lord Lovel is supposed to have concealed himself, the probability is that, unable to regain his
liberty, the neglect or treachery of a servant or
tenant brought about this tragic end.

A discovery of this nature was made in 1785
in a hidden vault at the foot of a stone
staircase at Brandon Hall, Suffolk.

Kingerby Hall, Lincolnshire, has a ghostly tradition of an unfortunate occupant of the hiding-hole near a fireplace being intentionally fastened in so that he was stifled with the heat and smoke ; the skeleton was found years afterwards in this horrible death-chamber.

Bayons Manor, in the same county, has some very curious arrangements for the sake of secretion and defence. There is a room in one of the barbican towers occupying its entire circumference, but so effectually hidden that its existence would never be suspected. In two of the towers are curious concealed stairs, and approaching " the Bishop's Tower " from the outer court or ballium, part of a flight of steps can be raised like a drawbridge to prevent sudden intrusion.[1]

A contributor to that excellent little journal *The Rambler*, unfortunately now extinct, mentions another very strange and weird device for security. " In the state-room of my castle," says the owner

[1] See Burke's *Visitation of Seats*, vol. i.

of this death-trap, " is the family shield, which on
a part being touched, revolves, and a flight of
steps becomes visible. The first, third, fifth, and
all odd steps are to be trusted, but to tread any
of the others is to set in motion some concealed
machinery which causes the staircase to collapse,
disclosing a vault some seventy feet in depth,
down which the unwary are precipitated."

At Tyttenhanger House, Hertfordshire, and in
the old manor house of Newport, Isle of Wight
(where the captive King Charles I. spent some
of his last melancholy days), there are rooms with
passages in the walls running completely round
them. Similar passages were found some years
ago while making alterations to Highclere Castle
Hampshire.

The once magnificent Madeley Court, Salop[1]
(now, alas! in the last stage of desolation and
decay, surrounded by coal-fields and undermined

[1] This house must not be confused with "the Upper House,"
connected with Charles II.'s wanderings.

by pits), is honeycombed with places for con-cealment and escape. A ruinous apartment at the top of the house, known as "the chapel" (only a few years ago wainscoted to the ceiling and divided by fine old oak screen), contained a secret chamber behind one of the panels. This could be fastened on the inside by a strong bolt. The walls of the mansion are of immense thickness, and the recesses and nooks noticeable everywhere were evidently at one time places of concealment ; one long triangular recess extends between two ruinous chambers (mere skeletons of past grandeur), and was no doubt for the purpose of reaching the basement from the first floor other than by the staircases. In the upper part of the house a dismal pit or well extends to the ground level, where it slants off in an oblique direction below the building, and terminates in a large pool or lake, after the fashion of that already described at Baddesley Clinton, in Warwickshire.

Everything points to the former magnificence

of this mansion ; the elaborate gate-house, the handsome stone porch, and even the colossal sundial, which last, for quaint design, can hold its own with those of the greatest baronial castles in Scotland. The arms of the Brooke family are to be seen emblazoned on the walls, a member of whom, Sir Basil, was he who christened the hunting-lodge of the Giffards " Boscobel," from the Italian words " bos co bello," on account of its woody situation. It is long since the Brookes migrated from Madeley—now close upon two centuries.

The deadly looking pits occasionally seen in ancient buildings are dangerous, to say the least of it. They may be likened to the shaft of our modern lift, with the car at the bottom and nothing above to prevent one from taking a step into eternity !

A friend at Twickenham sends us a curious account of a recent exploration of what was once the manor house, " Arragon Towers." We cannot do better than quote his words, written in answer to a request for particulars. " I did not," he says, " make sufficient examination of the hiding-place in the old manor house of Twickenham to give a detailed description of it, and I have no one here whom I could get to accompany me in exploring it now. It is not a thing to do by one's self, as one might make a false step, and have no one to assist in retrieving it. The entrance is in the top room of the one remaining turret by means of a movable panel in the wall opposite the window. The panel displaced, you see the top of a thick wall (almost on a line with the floor of the room). The width of the aperture is, I should think, nearly three feet ; that of the wall-top about a foot and a half ; the remaining space between the wall-top and the outer wall of the house is what you might perhaps term ' a chasm '—it is a sheer drop to the cellars of the house. I was told by the workmen that by walking the length of the wall-top (some fifteen feet) I should reach a stairway conducting to the vaults below, and that on reaching the bottom, a passage led off in the direction of the river, the tradition being that it actually went beneath the river to Ham House."

CHAPTER XII

HIDING-PLACES IN JACOBITE DWELLINGS
AND IN SCOTTISH CASTLES AND MANSIONS

DURING the Jacobite risings of 1715 and 1745 some of the "priest's holes" in the old Roman Catholic houses, especially in the north of England and in Scotland, came into requisition not only for storing arms and ammunition, but, after the failure of each enterprise, for concealing adherents of the luckless House of Stuart.

In the earlier mansion of Worksop, Nottinghamshire (burnt down in 1761), there was a large concealed chamber provided with a fireplace and a bed, which could only be entered by removing the sheets of lead forming the roofing. Beneath was a trap-door opening to a precipitous

flight of narrow steps in the thickness of a wall.
This led to a secret chamber, that had an inner
hiding-place at the back of a sliding panel.   A
witness in a trial succeeding " the '45 " declared
to having seen a large quantity of arms there
in readiness for the insurrection.

The last days of the notorious Lord Lovat
are associated with some of the old houses in
the north.   Cawdor Castle, Nairnshire, and Nether-
whitton, in Northumberland, claim the honour
of hiding this double-faced traitor prior to his
arrest.   At the former is a small chamber near the
roof, and in the latter is a hiding-place measuring
eight feet by three and ten feet high.   Nor must
be forgotten the tradition of Mistress Beatrice
Cope, behind the walls of whose bedroom Lovat
(so goes the story) was concealed, and the fugitive,
being asthmatical, would have revealed his whereabouts to the soldiers in search of him, had not
Mistress Cope herself kept up a persistent and
violent fit of coughing to drown the noise.

A secret room in the old Tudor house Ty
Mawr, Monmouthshire, is associated with the
Jacobite risings. It is at the back of " the parlour "
fireplace, and is entered through a square stone
slab at the foot of the staircase. The chamber
is provided with a small fireplace, the flue of
which is connected with the ordinary chimney, so
as to conceal the smoke. The same sort of
thing may be seen at Bisham Abbey, Berks.

Early in the last century a large hiding-place was
found at Danby Hall, Yorkshire. It contained
a large quantity of swords and pistols. Upon the
blade of each sword the word " shortly " was
engraved. Upwards of fifty sets of harness of
untanned leather of the early part of the eighteenth
century were further discovered, all of them in
so good a state of preservation that they were
afterwards used as cart-horse gear upon the farm.

No less than nine of the followers of " Bonnie
Prince Charlie " are said to have been concealed
in a secret chamber at Fetternear, Kemnay,

Aberdeenshire, an old seat of the Leslys of Balquhane. It was situated in the wall behind a large bookcase with a glazed front, a fixture in the room, the back of which could be made to slide back and give admittance to the recess.

Quite by accident an opening was discovered in a corner cupboard at an old house near Darlington. Certain alterations were in progress which necessitated the removal of the shelves, but upon this being attempted, they descended in some mysterious manner. The back of the cavity could then be pushed aside (that is to say, when the secret of its mechanism was discovered), and a hiding-place opened out to view. It contained some tawdry ornaments of Highland dress, which at one time, it was conjectured, belonged to an adherent of Prince Charlie.

The old mansion of Stonyhurst, Lancashire, contained many hiding-places. One of them, exactly like that at Fetternear, was at the back of a bookcase. A secret spring was discovered which opened a concealed door in the wall. In the space behind, a quantity of James II. guineas, a bed, and a mattress were found. A former student of this famous Jesuit college, who was instrumental in the discovery of a "priest's hole," has provided us with the following particulars : "It would be too long to tell you how I first discovered that in the floor of my bedroom, in the recess of the huge Elizabethan bay window, was a trap-door concealed by a thin veneering of oak ; suffice it to say that with a companion I devoted a delightful half-holiday to stripping off the veneering and breaking the lock of the trap-door. Between my floor and the ceiling of the long gallery below, was contrived a small room about five feet in height and the size and shape of the bay window recess. In one corner of this hiding-hole was what seemed a walled-up doorway, and it occurred to my companion and myself that we had heard some vague old tradition that all this part of the house was riddled with secret passages leading

from one concealed chamber to another, but
we did not seek to explore any farther." In
pulling down a portion of the college, a hollow
beam was discovered that opened upon concealed
hinges, used formerly for secreting articles of
value or sacred books and vessels ; and during
some alterations to the central tower, over the
main entrance to the mansion, a " priest's hole "
was found, containing seven horse pistols, ready
loaded and richly ornamented with silver, and—
a flask of rum ! A view could be obtained
from the interior of the hiding-place, in the
same manner as that which we have described
in the old summer-house at Salisbury ; a small
hole being devised in the design of the Sherburn
arms upon the marble shield over the gateway. This was the only provision for air and
light.

The quaint discovery of rum at Stonyhurst
suggests the story of a hiding-place in an old
house at Bishops Middleham, near Durham,

mentioned by Southey in his *Commonplace Book*. The house was occupied for years by a supposed total abstainer ; but a " priest's hole " in his bedroom, discovered after his death full of strong liquor, revealed the fact that by utilising the receptacle as a cellar he had been able to imbibe secretly to his heart's content.

A large quantity of Georgian gold coins were found some years ago in a small hiding-place under the oaken sill of a bedroom window at Gawthorp Hall, Lancashire, placed there, it is supposed, for the use of Prince Charles's army in passing through the country in 1745.

The laird of Belucraig (an old mansion in the parish of Aboyne, Aberdeenshire) was concealed after " the '45 " in his own house, while his wife, like the hostess of Chastleton, hospitably entertained the soldiers who were in search of him. The secret chamber where he was concealed was found some years ago in making some alterations to the roof. In it were a quantity of

Jacobite papers and a curious old arm-chair. The original entry was through a panel at the back of a " box bed " in the wainscot of a small, isolated bedroom at the top of the house. The room itself could only be reached by a secret staircase from a corridor below. The hiding-place was therefore doubly secure, and was a stronghold in case of greatest emergency. The Innes of Drumgersk and Belucraig were always staunch Roman Catholics and Jacobites. Their representatives lived in the old house until 1850.

In another old Aberdeenshire mansion, Dalpersie House, a hiding-hole or recess may be seen in one of the upper chambers, where was arrested a Gordon, one of the last victims executed after " the 45."

The ancient castles of Fyvie, Elphinstone, and Kemnay House have their secret chambers. The first of these is, with the exception of Glamis, perhaps, the most picturesque example of the tall-roofed and cone-topped turret style of architecture introduced from France in the days of James VI. A small space marked " the armoury " in an old plan of the building could in no way be accounted for, it possessing neither door, window, nor fireplace ; a trap-door, however, was at length found in the floor immediately above its supposed locality which led to its identification. At Kemnay (Aberdeenshire) the hiding-place is in the dining-room chimney ; and at Elphinstone (East Lothian), in the bay of a window of the great hall, is a masked entrance to a narrow stair in the thickness of the wall leading to a little room situated in the north-east angle of the tower ; it further has an exit through a trap-door in the floor of a passage in the upper part of the building.

The now ruinous castle of Towie Barclay, near Banff, has evidences of secret ways and con-trivances. Adjoining the fireplace of the great hall is a small room constructed for this purpose. In the wall of the same apartment is also a recess only to be reached by a narrow stairway in the thickness of the masonry, and approached from the flooring above the hall. A similar contrivance exists between the outer and inner walls of the dining hall of Carew Castle, Pembrokeshire.

Croxton Tower, near Elgin, contains a singular provision for communication from the top of the building to the basement, perfectly independent of the staircase. In the centre of each floor is a square stone which, when removed, reveals an opening from the summit to the base of the tower, through which a person could be lowered.

Another curious old Scottish mansion, famous for its secret chambers and passages, is Gordonstown. Here, in the pavement of a corridor in the west wing, a stone may be swung aside, beneath which is a narrow cell scooped out of one of the foundation walls. It may be followed to the adjoining angle, where it branches off into the next wall to an extent capable of holding fifty or sixty persons. Another large hiding-place is situated in one of the rooms at the back of a tall press or cupboard. The space in the wall is sufficiently large to contain eight or nine people, and entrance to it is effected by unloosing a spring bolt under the lower shelf, when the whole back of the press swings aside.

Whether the mystery of the famous secret room at Glamis Castle, Forfarshire, has ever been solved or satisfactorily explained beyond the many legends and stories told in connection with it, we have not been able to determine. The walls in this remarkable old mansion are in parts over twelve feet thick, and in them are several curious recesses, notably near the windows of the " stone hall." The secret chamber, or " Fyvie-room," as it is sometimes called, is said to have a window, which nevertheless has not led to the identification of its situation. Sir Walter Scott once slept a night at Glamis, and has described the " wild and straggling arrangement of the accommodation within doors." " I was conducted," he says,

" to my apartment in a distant corner of the building. I must own, as I heard door after door shut
after my conductor had retired, I began to con-
sider myself too far from the living and somewhat
too near the dead—in a word, I experienced sensa-
tions which, though not remarkable either for
timidity or superstition, did not fail to affect me
to the point of being disagreeable." We have
the great novelist's authority for saying that the
entrance of the secret chamber (in his time, at any
rate), by the law or custom of the family, could
only be known to three persons at once—*viz.* the
Earl of Strathmore, his heir-apparent, and any
third person whom they might take into their
confidence.

The great mystery of the secret chamber was
imparted to the heir of Glamis, or the heir-
presumptive, as the case might be, upon the eve
of his arriving at his majority, and thus it passed
into modern times from the dim and distant
feudal days. That the secret should be thus

handed down through centuries without being divulged is indeed remarkable, yet so is the story ; and many a time a future lord of Glamis has boasted that he would reveal everything when he should come of age. Still, however, when that time *did* arrive, in every case the recipient of the deadly secret has solemnly refused point blank to speak a word upon the subject.

There is a secret chamber at the old Cumberland seat of the ancient family of Senhouse. To this day its position is known only by the heir-at-law and the family solicitor. This room at Nether Hall is said to have no window, and has hitherto baffled every attempt of those not in the secret to discover its whereabouts.

Remarkable as this may seem in these prosaic days, it has been confirmed by the present representative of the family, who, in a communication to us upon the subject, writes as follows : " It may be romantic, but still it is true that the secret has survived frequent searches of visitors.

There is no one alive who has been in it, that I am aware, except myself." Brandeston Hall, Suffolk, is also said to have a hiding-place known only to two or three persons.

CHAPTER XIII

CONCEALED DOORS, SUBTERRANEAN
PASSAGES, ETC.

NUMEROUS old houses possess secret doors, passages, and staircases—Franks, in Kent; Eshe Hall, Durham; Binns House, Scotland; Dannoty Hall, and Whatton Abbey, Yorkshire; are examples. The last of these has a narrow flight of steps leading down to the moat, as at Baddesley Clinton. The old house Marks, near Romford, pulled down in 1808 after many years of neglect and decay—as well as the ancient seat of the Tichbournes in Hampshire, pulled down in 1803—and the west side of Holme Hall, Lancashire, demolished in the last century, proved to have been riddled with hollow walls. Secret doors and panels are still pointed out at Bramshill, Hants, (in the long gallery and billiard-room); in the long gallery at Penshurst; the oak room, Bochym House, Cornwall; the King's bedchamber, Ford Castle, Northumberland; the plotting-parlour of the White Hart Hotel, Hull; Low Hall, Yeadon, Yorkshire; Sawston; the Queen's chamber at Kimbolton Castle, Huntingdonshire, etc., etc.

A concealed door exists on the left-hand side of the fireplace of the gilt room of Holland House, Kensington, associated by tradition with the ghost of the first Lord Holland. Upon the authority of the Princess Lichtenstein, it appears there is, close by, a blood-stain which nothing can efface! It is to be hoped no enterprising person may be induced to try his skill here with the success that attended a similar attempt at Holyrood, as recorded by Scott![1]

In the King's writing-closet at Hampton Court may be seen the "secret door" by which

[1] *Vide* Introduction to *The Fair Maid of Perth.*

OLD WOODSTOCK PALACE, OXFORDSHIRE.
(*From an old Print.*)

MARKYATE CELL, HERTFORDSHIRE,

William III. left the palace when he wished to go out unobserved ; but this is more of a *private* exit than a *secret* one.

The old Château du Puits, Guernsey, has a hiding-hole placed between two walls which form an acute angle ; the one constituting part of the masonry of an inner courtyard, the other a wall on the eastern side of the main structure. The space between could be reached through the floor of an upper room.

Cousans, in his *History of Hertfordshire*, gives a curious account of the discovery of an iron door up the kitchen chimney of the old house Markyate Cell, near Dunstable. A short flight of steps led from it to another door of stout oak, which opened by a secret spring, and led to an unknown chamber on the ground level. Local tradition says this was the favourite haunt of a certain " wicked Lady Ferrers," who, disguised in male attire, robbed travellers upon the highway, and being wounded in one of these exploits, was discovered lying dead outside the walls of the house ; and the malignant nature of this lady's spectre is said to have had so firm a hold upon the villagers that no local labourer could be induced to work upon that particular part of the building.

Beare Park, near Middleham, Yorkshire, had a hiding-hole entered from the kitchen chimney, as had also the Rookery Farm, near Cromer ; West Coker Manor House; and The Chantry, at Ilminster, both in Somerset. At the last named, in another hiding-place in the room above, a bracket or credence-table was found, which is still preserved.

Many weird stories are told about Bovey House, South Devon, situated near the once notorious smuggling villages of Beer and Branscombe. Upon removing some leads of the roof a secret room was found, furnished with a chair and table. The well here is remarkable, and similar to that at Carisbrooke, with the exception that two people take the place of the donkey ! Thirty feet below the ground level there is said to have been a hiding-place—a large cavity cut in the solid rock. Many years ago a skeleton of a man was found at the bottom. Such dramatic material should suggest to some sensational novelist a tragic story, as the well and lime-walk at Ingatestone is said to have suggested *Lady Audley's Secret*.

A hiding-place something after the same style existed in the now demolished manor house of Besils Leigh, Berks. Down the shaft of a chimney a cavity was scooped out of the brickwork, to which a refugee had to be lowered by a rope. One of the towers of the west gate of Bodiam Castle contains a narrow square well in the wall leading to the ground level, and, as the guide was wont to remark, " how much farther the Lord only knows " ! This sort of thing may also be seen at Mancetter House, Warwickshire, and Ightham Moat, Kent, both approached by a staircase.

A communication formerly ran from a secret

chamber in the oak-panelled dining-room of Birts-
morton Court, Worcestershire, to a passage beneath
the moat that surrounds the structure, and thence
to an exit on the other side of the water.   During
the Wars of the Roses Sir John Oldcastle is said
to have been concealed behind the secret panel ;
but now the romance is somewhat marred, for
modern vandalism has converted the cupboard into
a repository for provisions.   The same indignity has
taken place at that splendid old timber house in
Cheshire, Moreton Hall, where a secret room,
provided with a sleeping-compartment, situated over
the kitchen, has been modernised into a repository
for the storing of cheeses.   From the hiding-
place the moat could formerly be reached, down
a narrow shaft in the wall.

Chelvey Court, near Bristol, contained two
hiding-places ; one, at the top of the house, was
formerly entered through a panel, the other (a
narrow apartment having a little window, and an
iron candle-holder projecting from the wall) through

PORCH AT CHELVEY COURT, SOMERSETSHIRE.

the floor of a cupboard.[1] Both the panel and
the trap-door are now done away with, and the
tradition of the existence of the secret rooms
almost forgotten, though not long since we received
a letter from an antiquarian who had seen them
thirty years before, and who was actually entertaining the idea of making practical investigations
with the aid of a carpenter or mason, to which,
as suggested, we were to be a party ; the idea,
however, was never carried out.

Granchester Manor House, Cambridgeshire,
until recently possessed three places of concealment.
Madingley Hall, in the same neighbourhood, has
two, one of them entered from a bedroom on
the first floor, has a space in the thickness of
the wall high enough for a man to stand upright
in it. The manor house of Woodcote, Hants,
also possessed two, which were each capable of
holding from fifteen to twenty men, but these repositories are now opened out into passages. One

[1] See *Notes and Queries*, September, 1855.

was situated behind a stack of chimneys, and contained an inner hiding-place. The "priests' quarters" in connection with the hiding-places are still to be seen.

Harborough Hall, Worcestershire, has two "priests' holes," one in the wall of the dining-room, the other behind a chimney in an upper room.

The old mansion of the Brudenells, in North-amptonshire, Deene Park, has a large secret chamber at the back of the fireplace in the great hall, sufficiently capacious to hold a score of people. Here also a hidden door in the panelling leads towards a subterranean passage running in the direction of the ruinous hall of Kirby, a mile and a half distant. In a like manner a passage extended from the great hall of Warleigh, an Elizabethan house near Plymouth, to an outlet in a cliff some sixty yards away, at whose base the tidal river flows.

Speke Hall, Lancashire (perhaps the finest specimen extant of the wood-and-plaster style of architecture nicknamed "Magpie"), formerly possessed a long underground communication extending from the house to the shore of the river Mersey ; a member of the Norreys family concealed a priest named Richard Brittain here in the year 1586, who, by this means, effected his escape by boat.

The famous secret passage of Nottingham Castle, by which the young King Edward III. and his loyal associates gained access to the fortress and captured the murderous regent and usurper Mortimer, Earl of March, is known to this day as " Mortimer's Hole." It runs up through the perpendicular rock upon which the castle stands, on the south-east side from a place called Brewhouse yard, and has an exit in what was originally the courtyard of the building. The Earl was seized in the midst of his adherents and retainers on the night of October 19th, 1330, and after a skirmish, notwithstanding the prayers and entreaties of his paramour Queen Isabella, he was bound and carried away through the passage in the rock, and shortly afterwards met his well-deserved death on the gallows at Smithfield.

But what ancient castle, monastery, or hall has not its traditional subterranean passage? Certainly the majority are mythical; still, there are some well authenticated. Burnham Abbey, Buckinghamshire, for example, or Tenterden Hall, Hendon, had passages which have been traced for over fifty yards; and one at Vale Royal, Nottinghamshire, has been explored for nearly a mile. In the older portions in both of the great wards of Windsor Castle arched passages thread their way below the basement, through the chalk, and penetrate to some depth below the site of the castle ditch at the base of the walls.[1] In the neighbourhood of Ripon subterranean passages have been found from time to time—tunnels of finely moulded masonry supposed to have been connected at one time with Fountains Abbey.

---

[1] See Marquis of Lorne's (Duke of Argyll) *Governor's Guide to Windsor*.

A passage running from Arundel Castle in the direction of Amberley has also been traced for some considerable distance, and a man and a dog have been lost in following its windings, so the entrance is now stopped up. About three years ago a long underground way was discovered at Margate, reaching from the vicinity of Trinity Church to the smugglers' caves in the cliffs ; also at Port Leven, near Helston, a long subterranean tunnel was discovered leading to the coast, no doubt very useful in the good old smuggling days. At Sunbury Park, Middlesex, was found a long vaulted passage some five feet high and running a long way under the grounds. Numerous other examples could be stated, among them at St. Radigund's Abbey, near Dover ; Liddington Manor House, Wilts ; the Bury, Rickmansworth ; "Sir Harry Vane's House," Hampstead, etc., etc.

CHAPTER XIV

MINIATURE HIDING-HOLES FOR
VALUABLES, ETC.

SMALL hidden recesses for the concealment of valuables or compromising deeds, etc., behind the wainscoting of ancient houses, frequently come to light. Many a curious relic has been discovered from time to time, often telling a strange or pathetic story of the past. A certain Lady Hoby, who lived at Bisham Abbey, Berkshire, is said by tradition to have caused the death of her little boy by too severe corporal punishment for his obstinacy in learning to write. A grim sequel to the legend happened not long since. Behind a window shutter in a small secret cavity in the wall was found an ancient, tattered copy-book, which, from the blots and its general slovenly appearance, was no doubt the handiwork of the unfortunate little victim to Lady Hoby's wrath.

When the old manor house of Wandsworth was pulled down recently, upon removing some old panelling a little cupboard was discovered, full of dusty phials and mouldy pill-boxes bearing the names of poor Queen Anne's numerous progeny who died in infancy.

Richard Cromwell spent many of his later years at Hursley, near Winchester, an old house now pulled down. In the progress of demolition what appeared to be a piece of rusty metal was found in a small cavity in one of the walls, which turned out to be no less important a relic than the seal of the Commonwealth of England.

Walford, in *Greater London*, mentions the discovery of some articles of dress of Elizabeth's time behind the wainscot of the old palace of Richmond, Surrey. Historical portraits have

frequently been found in this way. Behind the
panelling in a large room at the old manor
house of Great Gaddesden, Herts, were a number
of small aumbrys, or recesses. A most interesting
panel-portrait of Queen Elizabeth was found in
one of them, which was exhibited at the Tudor
Exhibition. In 1896, when the house of John
Wesley at Lewisham was pulled down, who
should be found between the walls but the
amorous Merry Monarch and a court beauty!
The former is said to be Riley's work. Secretary
Thurloe's MSS., as is well known, were found
embedded in a ceiling of his lodgings at Lincoln's
Inn. In pulling down a block of old buildings
in Newton Street, Holborn, a hidden space was
found in one of the chimneys, and there, covered
with the dust of a century, lay a silver watch,
a silk guard attached, and seals bearing the Lovat
crest. The relic was promptly claimed by Mr. John
Fraser, the claimant to the long-disputed peerage.[1]

[1] December 14th, 1895.

Small hiding-places have been found at the manor house of Chew Magna, Somerset, and Milton Priory, a Tudor mansion in Berkshire. In the latter a green shagreen case was found containing a seventeenth-century silver and ivory pocket knife and fork. A small hiding-place at Coughton Court, Warwickshire, brought to light a bundle of priest's clothes, hidden there in the days of religious persecution. In 1876 a small chamber was found at Sanderstead Court, Surrey, containing a small blue-and-white jar of Charles I.'s time. Three or four small secret repositories existed behind some elaborately carved oak panels in the great hall of the now ruinous Harden Hall, near Stockport. In similar recesses at Gawdy Hall, Suffolk, were discovered two ancient apostle spoons, a watch, and some Jacobean MSS. A pair of gloves and some jewels of seventeenth-century date were brought to light not many years ago in a secret recess at Woodham Mortimer Manor House, Essex.

A very curious example of a hiding-place for
valuables formerly existed at an old building
known as Terpersie Castle, near Alford, Lincolnshire. The sides of it were lined with stone to
preserve articles from damp, and it could be
drawn out of the wall like a drawer.

In the year 1861 a hidden receptacle was found
at the Elizabethan college of Wedmore, Kent, containing Roman Catholic MSS. and books ; and at
Bromley Palace, close by, in a small aperture below
the floor, was found the leathern sole of a pointed
shoe of the Middle Ages ! Small hiding-places of
this nature existed in a wing, now pulled down,
of the Abbey House, Whitby (in "Lady Anne's
Room"). At Castle Ashby, Northants ; Fountains
Hall, near Ripon ; Ashes House, near Preston ;
Trent House, Somerset ; and Ockwells, Berks,[1] are
panels opening upon pivots and screening small
cavities in the walls.

---

[1] Another hiding-place is said to have existed behind the fireplace of the hall.

HURSTMONCEAUX CASTLE, SUSSEX

CHAPTER XV

HIDING-PLACES OF SMUGGLERS AND THIEVES

HORSFIELD, in his *History of Sussex*, gives a curious account of the discovery in 1738 of an iron chest in a recess of a wall at the now magnificent ruin Hurstmonceaux Castle. In the thickness of the walls were many curious staircases communicating with the galleries. When the old castle was allowed to fall into ruin, the secret passages, etc., were used by smugglers as a convenient receptacle for contraband goods.

Until recently there was an ingenious hiding-place behind a sliding panel at the old "Bell Inn" at Sandwich which had the reputation of having formerly been put to the same use; indeed, in many

another old house near the coast were hiding-
places utilised for a like purpose.

In pulling down an old house at Erith in 1882
a vault was discovered with strong evidence that
it had been extensively used for smuggling. The
pretty village of Branscombe, on the Devonshire
coast, was, like the adjacent village of Beer, a notorious place for smugglers. "The Clergy House,"
a picturesque, low-built Tudor building (condemned as being insecure and pulled down a few
years ago), had many mysterious stories told of its
former occupants, its underground chambers and
hiding-places ; indeed, the villagers went so far as
to declare that there was *another house* beneath
the foundations !

A secret chamber was discovered at the back
of a fireplace in an old house at Deal, from
which a long underground passage extended to
the beach. The house was used as a school,
and the unearthly noises caused by the wind
blowing up this smugglers' passage created much

consternation among the young lady pupils. A lady of our acquaintance remembers, when a schoolgirl at Rochester, exploring part of a vaulted tunnel running in the direction of the castle from Eastgate House, which in those days was a school, and had not yet received the distinction of being the "Nun's House" of *Edwin Drood*. Some way along, the passage was blocked by the skeleton of a donkey! Our informant is not given to romancing, therefore we must accept the story in good faith.

All round the coast-line of Kent once famous smuggling buildings are still pointed out. Movable hollow beams have been found supporting cottage ceilings, containing all kinds of contraband goods. In one case, so goes the story, a customs house officer in walking through a room knocked his head, and the tell-tale hollow sound (from the beam, not from his head, we will presume) brought a discovery. At Folkestone, tradition says, a long row of houses used for the purpose

13

had the cellars connected one with the other right the way along, so that the revenue officers could be easily evaded in the case of pursuit.

The modern utility of a convenient secret panel or trap-door occasionally is apparent from the police-court reports. The tenements in noted thieves' quarters are often found to have inter-communication; a masked door will lead from one house to the other, and trap-doors will enable a thief to vanish from the most keen-sighted detective, and nimbly thread his way over the roofs of the neighbouring houses. There was a case in the papers not long since; a man, being closely chased, was on the point of being seized, when, to the astonishment of his pursuers, he suddenly disappeared at a spot where apparently he had been closely hemmed in.

Many old houses in Clerkenwell were, sixty or seventy years ago, notorious thieves' dens, and were noted for their hiding-places, trap-doors, etc., for evading the vigilance of the law. The name of Jack Sheppard, as may be supposed, had connection with the majority. One of these old buildings had been used in former years as a secret Jesuits' college, and the walls were threaded with masked passages and places of concealment ; and when the old " Red Lion Inn " in West Street was pulled down in 1836, some artful traps and false floors were discovered which tarried well with its reputation as a place of rendezvous and safety for outlaws. The " Rising Sun " in Holywell Street is a curious example, there being many false doors and traps in various parts of the house ; also in the before-mentioned Newton Street a panel could be raised by a pulley, through which a fugitive or outlaw could effect his escape on to the roof, and thence into the adjoining house.

One of the simplest and most secure hiding-places perhaps ever devised by a law-breaker was that within a water-butt ! A cone-shaped repository, entered from the bottom, would allow a man

to sit within it ; nevertheless, to all intents and
purposes the butt was kept full of water, and
could be apparently emptied from a tap at its
base, which, of course, was raised from the
ground to admit the fugitive. We understand
such a butt is still in existence somewhere in
Yorkshire.

A " secret staircase " in Partingdale House,
Mill Hill, is associated (by tradition) with the
notorious Dick Turpin, perhaps because of its
proximity to his haunts upon Finchley Common.
As it exists now, however, there is no object
for secrecy, the staircase leading merely to the
attics, and its position can be seen ; but the
door is well disguised in a Corinthian column
containing a secret spring. Various alterations
have taken place in this house, so once upon a
time it may have had a deeper meaning than is
now perceptible.

Another supposed resort of this famous high-
wayman is an old ivy-grown cottage at Thornton

BOVEY HOUSE, SOUTH DEVON.

MAPLEDURHAM HOUSE, OXFORDSHIRE.

Heath. Narrow steps lead up from the open chimney towards a concealed door, from which again steps descend and lead to a subterranean passage having an exit in the garden.

We do not intend to go into the matter of modern secret chambers, and there are such things, as some of our present architects and builders could tell us, for it is no uncommon thing to design hiding-places for the security of valuables. For instance, we know of a certain suburban residence, built not more than thirty years ago, where one of the rooms has capacities for swallowing up a man six feet high and broad in proportion. We have known such a person—or shall we say victim ?—to appear after a temporary absence, of say, five minutes, with visible signs of discomfort ; but as far as we are aware the secret is as safe in his keeping as is the famous mystery in the possession of the heir of Glamis.

An example of a sliding panel in an old house in Essex (near Braintree) was used as a pattern for the entrance to a modern secret chamber ;[1] and no doubt there are many similar instances where the ingenuity of our ancestors has thus been put to use for present-day requirements.

Our collection of houses with hiding-holes is now coming to an end. We will briefly summarise those that remain unrecorded.

" New Building " at Thirsk has, or had, a secret chamber measuring three feet by six. Upon the outside wall on the east side of the house is a small aperture into which a stone fitted with such nicety that no sign of its being movable could possibly be detected ; at the same time, it could be removed with the greatest ease in the event of its being necessary to supply a person in hiding with food.

Catledge Hall, Cambridgeshire, has a small

---

[1] According to the newspaper reports, the recently recovered " Duchess of Devonshire," by Gainsborough, was for some time secreted behind a secret panel in a sumptuous steam-launch up the river Thames, from whence it was removed to America in a trunk with a false bottom.

MAPLEDURHAM HOUSE, OXFORDSHIRE.

ENTRANCE TO SECRET STAIRCASE, PARTINGDALE HOUSE, MILL HILL.

octangular closet adjoining a bedroom, from which formerly there was a secret way on to the leads of the roof.

At Dunkirk Hall, near West Bromwich, is a "priest's hole" in the upper part of the house near "the chapel," which is now divided into separate rooms.

Mapledurham House, Oxon, the old seat of the Blounts, contains a "priest's hole" in the attics, descent into which could be made by the aid of a rope suspended for that purpose.

Upton Court, near Slough, possesses a "priest's hole," entered from a fireplace, provided with a double flue—one for smoke, the other for ventilation to the hiding-place.

Knebworth House, Hertfordshire, formerly had a secret chamber known as "Hell Hole."

Eastgate House, Rochester (before mentioned), has a hiding-place in one of the upstairs rooms. It has, however, been altered.

Milsted Manor, Kent, is said to have a secret

exit from the library ; and Sharsted Court (some three miles distant) has a cleverly marked panel in the wainscoting of "the Tapestry Dressing-room," which communicates by a very narrow and steep flight of steps in the thickness of the wall with "the Red Bedroom."

The "Clough Inn" at Chard, Somersetshire, is said by tradition to have three secret rooms !

Cawdor Castle, Nairnshire—a hiding-place formerly in "the tower." Bramhall Hall, Cheshire —two secret recesses were discovered not long ago during alterations. The following also contain hiding-places : — Hall-i'-the-wood, Bolling Hall, Mains Hall, and Huncoat Hall, all in Lancashire ; Drayton House, Northants; Packington Old Hall, Warwickshire ; Batsden Court, Salop ; Melford Hall, Suffolk ; Fyfield House, Wilts ; "New Building," Southwater, Sussex ; Barsham Rectory, Suffolk ; Porter's Hall, Southend, Essex ; Kirkby Knowle Castle and Barnborough Hall, Yorkshire ; Ford House, Devon ; Cothele, Cornwall ;

Hollingbourne Manor House, Kent (altered of late years) ; Salisbury Court, near Shenley, Herts.

Of hiding-places and secret chambers in the ancient castles and mansions upon the Continent we know but little.

Two are said to exist in an old house in the Hradschin in Prague—one communicating from the foundation to the roof " by a windlass or turn-pike." A subterranean passage extends also from the house beneath the street and the cathedral, and is said to have its exit in the Hirch Graben, or vast natural moat which bounds the château upon the north.

A lady of our acquaintance remembers her feeling of awe when, as a school-girl, she was shown a hiding-place in an old mansion near Baden-Baden— a huge piece of stone masonry swinging aside upon a pivot and revealing a gloomy kind of dungeon behind.

The old French châteaux, according to Froisart, were rarely without secret means of escape. King

Louis XVI., famous for his mechanical skill, manufactured a hiding-place in an inner corridor of his private apartments at the Palace of Versailles. The wall where it was situated was painted to imitate large stones, and the grooves of the opening were cleverly concealed in the shaded representations of the divisions. In this a vast collection of State papers was preserved prior to the Revolution.[1]

Mr. Lang tells us, in his admirable work *Pickle the Spy*, that Bonnie Prince Charlie, between the years 1749 and 1752, spent much of his time in the convent of St. Joseph in the Rue St. Dominique, in the Faubourg St. Germain, which under the late Empire (1863) was the hotel of the Minister of War. Here he appears to have been continually lurking behind the walls, and at night by a secret staircase visiting his protectress Madame de Vassés. Allusion is made in the same work to a secret

[1] Vide *The Memoirs of Madame Campan.*

cellar with a "dark stair" leading to James III.'s furtive audience-chamber at his residence in Rome.

So recently as the year 1832 a hiding-place in an old French house was put to practical use by the Duchesse de Berry after the failure of her enterprise to raise the populace in favour of her son the Duc de Bordeaux. She had, however, to reveal herself in preference to suffocation, a fire, either intentionally or accidentally, having been ignited close to where she was hidden, recalling the terrible experiences of Father Gerard at "Braddocks."

CHAPTER XVI

THE SCOTTISH HIDING-PLACES OF PRINCE CHARLES EDWARD

THE romantic escapes of Prince Charles Edward are somewhat beyond the province of this book, owing to the fact that the hiding-places in which he lived for the greater part of five months were not artificial but natural formations in the wild, mountainous country of the Western Highlands. Far less convenient and comfortable were these caves and fissures in the rocks than those secret places which preserved the life of the " young chevalier's " great-uncle Charles II. Altogether, the terrible hardships to which the last claimant to the Stuart throne was subjected were far greater in every way, and we can but admire the remarkable spirit, fortitude, and courage that carried him through his numerous dangers and trials.

The wild and picturesque character not only of the Scotch scenery, but of the loyal High-landers, who risked their all to save their King, gives the story of this remarkable escape a romantic colouring that surpasses any other of its kind, whether real or fictitious.

This, therefore, is our excuse for giving a brief summary of the Prince's wanderings, if only to add to our other hiding-places a record of the names of the isolated spots which have become historical landmarks.

In his flight from the fatal battlefield of Culloden the young Prince, when about four miles from Inverness, hastily determined to make the best of his way towards the western coast. The first halt was made at Castle Dounie, the seat of the crafty old traitor Lord Lovat. A hasty meal having been taken here, Charles and his little cavalcade of followers pushed on to Invergarry, where the chieftain, Macdonnell of Glengarry, otherwise "Pickle the Spy,"[1] being absent from home, an empty house was the only welcome, but the best was made of the situation. Here the bulk of the Prince's companions dispersed to look after their own safety, while he and one or two chosen friends continued the journey to Glenpean, the residence of the chieftain Donald Cameron. From Mewboll, which was reached the next night, the fugitives proceeded on foot to Oban, where a hovel was found for sleeping-quarters. In the village of Glenbiasdale, in Arisaig, near to where Charles had landed on his disastrous enterprise, he learned that a number of Royalist cruisers were upon the alert all along the coast, whereupon he determined to watch his opportunity and get across to the Western Isles, and remain concealed until a French vessel could be found to take him abroad.

[1] *Vide* Andrew Lang's *Pickle the Spy*.

A boat was procured, and the little party safely embarked, but in the voyage encountered such heavy seas that the vessel very nearly foundered; a landing, however, being effected at a place called Roonish, in the Isle of Benbecula, a habitation had to be made out of a miserable hut. Two days being thus wretchedly spent, a move was made to the Island of Scalpa, where Charles was entertained for four days in the house of Donald Campbell.

Meanwhile, a larger vessel was procured, the object being to reach Stornoway; but the inclemency of the weather induced Charles and his guide Donald Macleod to make the greater part of the journey by land. Arriving there hungry, worn out, and drenched to the skin, the Prince passed the night at Kildun, the house of Mrs. Mackenzie; an alarm of danger, however, forced him to sea again with a couple of companions, O'Sullivan and O'Neal; but shortly after they had embarked they sighted some men-of-war, so put to land once more at the Island of Jeffurt. Four days were passed away in this lonely spot, when the boat put out to sea once more, and after many adventures and privations the travellers landed at Loch Wiskaway, in Benbecula, and made their headquarters some two miles inland at a squalid hut scarcely bigger than a pigstye.

The next move was to an isolated locality named Glencorodale, in the centre of South Uist, where in a hut of larger dimensions the Prince held his court in comparative luxury, his wants being well looked after by Sir Alexander and Lady Macdonald and other neighbouring Jacobites. With thirty thousand pounds reward offered for his capture, and the Western Isles practically surrounded by the enemy, it is difficult to imagine the much-sought-for prize coolly passing his weary hours in fishing and shooting, yet such was the case for the whole space of a month.

An eye-witness describes Charles's costume at this time as "a tartan short coat and vest of the same, got from Lady Clanranald; his night-cap all patched with soot-drops, his shirt, hands, and face patched with the same; a short kilt, tartan hose, and Highland brogs."

From South Uist the fugitive removed to the Island of Wia, where he was received by Ranald Macdonald; thence he visited places called Rossinish and Aikersideallich, and at the latter had to sleep in a fissure in the rocks. Returning once more to South Uist, Charles (accompanied by O'Neal and Mackechan) found a hiding-place up in the hills, as the militia appeared to be dangerously near, and at night tramped towards Benbecula, near to which another place of safety was found in the rocks.

The memorable name of Flora Macdonald now appears upon the scene. After much scheming and many difficulties the meeting of the Prince and this noble lady was arranged in a squalid hut near Rosshiness. The hardships encountered upon the journey from Benbecula to this village

14

were some of the worst experiences of the unfortunate wanderer ; and when his destination
was reached at last, he had to be hurried off
again to a hiding-place by the sea-shore, which
provided little or no protection from the driving
torrents of rain. Early each morning this precaution had to be taken, as the Royalist soldiers,
who were quartered only a quarter of a mile
distant, repaired to the hut every morning to
get milk from the woman who acted as Charles's
hostess. Upon the third day after the Prince
had arrived, Flora Macdonald joined him, bring-
ing with her the disguise for the character he
was to impersonate upon a proposed journey to
the Isle of Skye—*viz.* " a flowered linen gown,
a light-coloured quilted petticoat, a white apron,
and a mantle of dun camlet, made after the
Irish fashion, with a hood."

A boat lay in readiness in a secluded nook
on the coast, and " Betty Burke "—the pseudo
servant-maid—Flora Macdonald, and Mackechan,

as guide, embarked and got safely to Kilbride, in Skye. Not, however, without imminent dangers. A storm nearly swamped the boat; and upon reaching the western coast of the island they were about to land, when a number of militiamen were noticed on shore, close at hand, and as they recognised their peril, and pulled away with might and main, a volley of musketry would probably have had deadly effect, had not the fugitives thrown themselves at the bottom of the boat.

At the house of the Macdonalds of Mugstat, whose representative dreaded the consequences of receiving Charles, another Macdonald was introduced as an accomplice by the merest accident. This staunch Jacobite at once took possession of " Betty," and hurried off towards his house of Kingsburgh. Upon the way the ungainly appearance of Flora's maid attracted the attention of a servant, who remarked that she had never seen such an impudent-looking woman. " See what

long strides the jade takes!'" she cried ; "and
how awkwardly she manages her petticoats!'"
And this was true enough, for in fording a
little brook "Betty Burke" had to be severely
reprimanded by her chaperon for her impropriety
in lifting her skirts! Upon reaching the house,
Macdonald's little girl caught sight of the strange
woman, and ran away to tell her mother that
her father had brought home "the most old,
muckle, ill-shapen-up wife" she had ever
seen. Startling news certainly for the lady of
Kingsburgh!

The old worn-out boots of the Prince's were
discarded for new ones ere he departed, and
fragments of the former were long afterwards worn
in the bosoms of Jacobite ladies.

The next step in this wonderful escape was to
Portree, where temporary accommodation was found
in a small public-house. Here Charles separated
from his loyal companions Neil Mackechan and the
immortal Flora. The "Betty Burke" disguise was

discarded and burnt and a Highland dress donned. With new guides the young Chevalier now made his headquarters for a couple of days or so in a desolate shepherd's hut in the Isle of Raasay; thence he journeyed to the north coast of the Isle of Skye, and near Scorobreck housed himself in a cow-shed. At this stage of his journey Charles altered his disguise into that of a servant of his then companion Malcolm Macleod, and at the home of his next host (a Mackinnon of Ellagol) was introduced as " Lewie Caw," the son of a surgeon in the Highland army. By the advice of the Mackinnons, the fugitive decided to return, under their guidance, again to the mainland, and a parting supper having been held in a cave by the sea-shore, he bid adieu to the faithful Macleod. The crossing having been effected, not without innumerable dangers, once more Charles found himself near the locality of his first landing. For the next three days neither cave nor hut dwelling could be found that was considered safe ; and

upon the fourth day, in exploring the shores of
Loch Nevis for a hiding-place, the fugitives ran
their little craft right into a militia boat that was
moored to and screened from view by a projecting
rock. The soldiers on land immediately sprang
on board and gave chase ; but with his usual good
luck Charles got clear away by leaping on land
at a turn of the lake, where his retreat was covered
by dense foliage.

After this the Prince was under the care
of the Macdonalds, one of which clan, Macdonald of Glenaladale, together with Donald
Cameron of Glenpean, took the place of the
Mackinnons.

A brief stay was made at Morar Lake and at
Borrodaile (both houses of the Macdonalds) ;
after which a hut in a wood near the latter place
and an artfully constructed hiding-place between
two rocks with a roof of green turf did service
as the Prince's palace.

In this cave Charles received the alarming news

that the Argyllshire Militia were on the scent, and were forming an impenetrable cordon completely round the district. Forced once more to seek refuge in flight, the unfortunate Stuart was hurried away through some of the wildest mountainous country he had yet been forced to traverse. A temporary hiding-place was found, and from this a search-party exploring the adjacent rocks and crags was watched with breathless interest.

Still within the military circle, a desperate dash for liberty had now to be planned. Nearly starved and reduced to the last extremity of fatigue, Charles and his guides, Glenpean and Glenaladale, crept stealthily upon all-fours towards the watch-fires, and taking advantage of a favourable moment when the nearest sentry was in such a position that their approach could be screened by the projecting rocks, in breathless silence the three stole by, and offering up a prayer for their deliverance, continued their foot-sore

journey until their legs would carry them no
farther.

The next four days Charles sought shelter
in caves in the neighbourhood of Glenshiel,
Strathcluanie, and Strathglass ; but the most
romantic episode in his remarkable adventures
was the sojourn in the secret caves and hiding-
places of the notorious robbers of Glenmoriston,
under whose protection the royal fugitive placed
himself.   With these wild freebooters he
continued for three weeks, during which time he
made himself extremely popular by his freedom
of intercourse with them.

The wanderer left these dwellings of comparative
luxury that he might join hands with other fugitive
Jacobites, Macdonald of Lochgarry and Cameron
of Clunes, and took up his quarters in the wood-
surrounded huts near Loch Arkaig and Auchnacarry.

The poor youth's appearance at this period is
thus described by one of his adherents : " The
Prince was at this time bare-footed, had an old

black kilt-coat on, philabeg and waistcoat, a dirty shirt, and a long red beard, a gun in his hand, and a pistol and dirk by his side."

Moving again to miserable hovels in the wild recesses of the mountain Benalder, the chieftains Lochiel and Cluny acted now as the main body-guard. The former of these two had devised a very safe hiding-place in the mountain which went by the name of "the Cage," and while here welcome news was brought that two friendly vessels had arrived at Lochnanuagh, their mission being,· if possible, to seek out and carry away the importunate heir to the Stuart throne.

The last three or four days of Charles's memorable adventures were occupied in reaching Glencamger, halts being made on the day at Corvoy and Auchnacarry. On Saturday, September 20th, 1746, he was on board *L'Heureux*, and nine days later landed at Roscoff, near Morlaix.

So ended the famous escapades of the young Chevalier Prince Charles Edward.

Here is a fine field open to some enterprising artistic tourist. How interesting it would be to follow Prince Charles throughout his journeyings in the Western Highlands, and illustrate with pen and pencil each recorded landmark! Not long since Mr. Andrew Lang gave, in a weekly journal (*The Sketch*), illustrations of the most famous of all the Prince's hiding-places—*viz.* the cave in Glenmoriston, Inverness-shire.[1] The cave, we are told, is "formed like a tumulus by tall boulders, but is clearly a conspicious object, and a good place wherein to hunt for a fugitive. But it served its turn, and as another cave in the same district two miles off is lost, perhaps it is not so conspicious as it seems." It is about twenty feet wide at the base, and the position of the hearth and the royal bed are still to be seen, with "the finest purling stream that could be, running by the bed-side." How handy for the morning "tub"!

[1] They appeared originally in Blaikie's *Itinerary of Prince Charles Stuart* (Scottish History Society).

In that remarkable collection of Stuart relics on exhibition in 1889 were many pathetic mementoes of Charles's wanderings in the Highlands. Here could be seen not only the mittens but the chemise of " Betty Burke " ; the punch-bowl over which the Prince and the host of Kingsburgh had a late carousal, and his Royal Highness's table-napkins used in the same hospitable house ; a wooden coffee-mill, which provided many a welcome cup of coffee in the days of so many hardships ; a silver dessert-spoon, given to Dr. Macleod by the fugitive when he left the Isle of Skye ; the Prince's pocket-book, many of his pistols, and a piece of his Tartan disguise ; a curious relic in the form of two lines of music, sent as a warning to one of his lurking-places—when folded in a particular way the following words become legible, "Conceal yourself; your foes look for you." There was also a letter from Charles saying he had " arrived safe aboard ye vessell " which carried him to France, and numerous little things which gave the history of the escape remarkable reality.

The recent dispersal of the famous Culloden collection sent long-cherished Jacobite relics broadcast over the land. The ill-fated Stuart's bed and walking-stick were of course the plums of this sale ; but they had no connection with the Highland wanderings after the battle. The only object that had any connection with the story was the gun of *L'Heureux*.

We understand there is still a much-prized heirloom now in Glasgow—a rustic chair used by the Prince when in Skye. The story is that, secreted in one of his cave dwellings, he espied a lad in his immediate vicinity tending some cows. Hunger made him reveal himself, with the result that he was taken to the boy's home, a farm not far off, and had his fill of cream and oatcakes, a delicacy which did not often fall in his way. The visit naturally was repeated ; and long afterwards, when the rank of his guest came to the knowledge of the good farmer, the royal chair was promoted from its old corner in the kitchen to an honoured position worthy of such a valued possession.

THE END.

INDEX

Printed by Hazell, Watson & Viney, Ld., London and Aylesbury.

www.ingramcontent.com/pod-product-compliance
Lightning Source LLC
LaVergne TN
LVHW051727080426
835511LV00018B/2916